PONTIUS

Redeemed

™

By

Mark Darby Slater

15th June 2025

SPECIAL EDITION

Biblical References in Context

No part of this book may be reproduced in any form without the express written consent of the author.

All rights reserved. 2020. Revised Editions 2023, 2024

1

DEDICATIONS

My late mother Glennis May
My late father William Thomas
(aka Mog Mason, Champion of Wales)

My sisters Christine & Caroline

Marissa & Toby

Friends, "my brothers & sisters in Yeshua,"

Terry, Chancey & the late Harry

"My Creative Team" & All my Patrons

Trevor John Keates,
16th December 1947 - 31st July 2023

CONTENTS

4		PRINCIPAL CHARACTERS
5		TAVAK – Into the Midst
11	Chapter 1 –	DEPARTURE
23	Chapter 2 –	PROCESSION
31	Chapter 3 –	OCCUPIED LAND
33	Chapter 4 –	GRAVEN IMAGES
44	Chapter 5 -	SIT DOWN
60	Chapter 6 –	FORGIVENESS & HEALING
74	Chapter 7 –	PLOT
77	Chapter 8 –	COMPETITION
86	Chapter 9 –	PROCESSIONS
93	Chapter 10 –	TEMPLE
99	Chapter 11 –	VISION
103	Map -	*Jerusalem*
104	Chapter 12 –	TRIAL
138	Figurative -	*Portraiture*
149	Chapter 13 –	DEATH
162	Chapter 14 –	THEFT
178	Chapter 15 –	SEARCH
191	Chapter 16 –	AQUEDUCT
203	Chapter 17 –	MASSACRE
218	Chapter 18 –	EMPEROR GOD
233	Chapter 19 –	TORTURE
246	Chapter 20 –	ASSASSINATION
251	Chapter 21 –	SAVIOR

264 – ACKNOWLEDGEMENTS, 265 – SOURCES, 264 – EPILOGUES, 267 -ART DEPARTMENT, 271 - NO MAN CALLED ME, 271- LINKS & AN APPEAL, 273 - SCREENPLAY REVIEWS, 275 – RAINBOW SLICKY SLIDE, 276 - CAST OF CHARACTERS, 278 - BOOK REVIEWS, 280 - CHRIST FOR THE NATIONS, 282 – AUTHOR'S NOTES, 283 - THE MEANING, 284 – BIBLIOGRAPHY, 295 - PONTIUS STORY BOARDS BY MONTGOMERY TRIZ, 308 – CAROFINEART.CO.UK FIGURATIVE , 312 – AFFIRMATION, WRITING PONTIUS.

PRINCIPAL CHARACTERS
in order of appearance

Antonius	Centurion, Claudia's cousin
Lefus	Centurion,
Pontius Pilate	The Roman Prefect
Yeshua Ha Mashiach	Jesus the Messiah
Barabbas	Leader of the Sicarii
Dominicus	Paramour
Mus	Pontius's groom
Claudia Procula	Pontius's wife
Gaius Caligula	Tiberius Caesar's nephew
Tiberius	Caesar
Vinicianus	Senator
Caiaphas	The Temple High Priest
Shira	Hebrew servant
Annas	The Former Chief Priest
Nicodemus	Pharisee
Joseph of Arimathea	Pharisee

A complete list appears in the Appendix on page 276.

TAVAK - "Into the Midst"

Morning, Wednesday, April 28th 28 CE
(The Chronological Gospels page 235)

ANTONIA FORTRESS, JERUSALEM

A buzz of atmospheric noise; some flies, indecipherable mutterings from the apprehensive crowd. Dust settles around the sandaled feet of the stoic soldiers. This first wave of Romans back-up to the walls. In unison, with a burst of energy, draw ear-grating scraping swords from scabbards with a show of glistening metal force. Shiny thick leather breast plates, brown tunics, leather skirts, helmets with plumes removed for battle. They stand in sharp opposition to the drab, earth-toned civilian garments of the ordinary Judean mob facing them. The volume of noises decreases as more dust descends. The crowd, know well the brutality of this conquering force, grows ever more silent.

Centurions Antonius and Lefus, with uniform embellishments of rank, peer down from the top of a wall to watch their cohort. More soldiering men, one hundred and fifty, ominously continue to march slowly to the face of the fortress walls at ground level.

Their presence has been ordered by Pontius Pilate, The Prefect of Judea and Samaria, as a counterforce to the growing unrest which threatens his peace and quiet. Pontius appears at the top of the wall and strides purposefully to its edge. His arrival accentuates the eerie silence as the apprehensive crowd wonders what his next command will be. They have heard about his compassion. The brave Hebrew people would've laid down their lives for their beliefs and superstitions, but Pontius mercifully forgave them. That perceived weakness may well work against him today. Pontius, a determined man, looks with disdain at the insubordination of the masses. They waste his time. They smell like beasts of burden, or worse, for having travelled without a bath. Their garments are ragged; hair and beards are unkempt. Yet the anonymous voices within the rabble mumble again.

"Barabbas".

The top of the wall, like a plinth, is a high cap to the stone castle built by Herod the Great. Called The Antonia Fortress, named to honor Herod's friend, the Roman, Mark Anthony. This huge structure covers the high ground above Jerusalem. Dominating the north-west corner of the Temple Mount, but not as grand as the Temple itself, it serves as a barracks, an exercise courtyard, and a defendable structure. It symbolizes the pandering of a tetrarch to his rulers.

The late King Herod, part-Hebrew, part-Arab, part politician, full-time opportunistic friend of Rome, owned three palaces, now inherited by his sons, Antipas and Agrippa. The offspring know how to prosper during this oppressive Roman rule. Political cunning and social climbing in the city of Rome have been rewarded. Herod Antipas, desiring friendship with the Roman Prefect, has offered him two palaces. The royal residence on the eastern end of the Mediterranean Sea, Caesarea Marittima and one in the city of Jerusalem. Pontius claims the smaller palace in Jerusalem, which is nearer to the Antonia Fortress. Pontius and his wife Claudia would prefer to be on the seashore some two days ride away from Jerusalem.

The Romanesque Pontius, short, stocky, in his midlife, near the end of that very peak of physical fitness, walks from the edge of the wall to sit down in a rock-solid chair. The quiet gives him time for serious thought. The mass of people below looks expectant, waits, but the tension can hold no longer. Silence breaks again as murmuring ripples and mumblings recommence. Isolated shouts pierce the atmosphere.

"Barabbas."

Pilgrims and residents chatter among themselves. A few weaves mingle, and whisper. A group of well-dressed men cling together. These anonymous gossipers may shove an unsuspecting individual to gain attention or intimidate.

The few Roman soldiers who stand around on top of the wall seek, with nervous darting eyes, orders and direction. The Prefect ponders all this while the Centurion Antonius (cousin to Claudia, the Prefect's wife) gazes down at the slow in-coming masses. Antonius raises his line of sight above the heads of the mob to imagine in the distance the many thousands of pilgrims journeying to the city for their annual Passover celebration. Some of the rabble looks up to him expectantly as if they know something more about this man.

Antonius, a young man of fine Roman features, has a look of concern that makes him appear different to his fellow Romans. He finds conflict lies deep within. So internal it transfixes him, makes him impotent. The miracle worker, Yeshua Ha Mashiach, who saved Antonius's servant, stands just feet away. Centurion Lefus, with an aggressive stride, arrives to observe from this vantage point. His eyes look like pins of light surrounded by darkness. His battle-scarred face adds beauty to an otherwise ugly plainness.

Pontius observes the increasing trickle of people from outside the wall like the gradual flow when the sluice of a new aqueduct actively opens for the first time. His desire is for water in Jerusalem, his plan for two aqueducts. Not this growing dirty human tide which diverts his energy. His time should be spent on improved Roman engineering to bring more fresh water to the city, not in this labor of contention.

"Barabbas, Barabbas, Barabbas."

Pontius sets his jaw. He knows what they want. The injustice of their demand wriggles inside him like some filthy maggot that passed his lips disguised in undercooked pork. The situation becomes more distasteful each passing second. The Prefect knows where the evidence against the innocent man, Yeshua, comes from. It comes from envy. This peaceful prince has been deserted by the throngs that threw palms at his feet the week before. Where are those adoring multitudes now?

Dressed in fine clothes, head covered and adorned, with interwoven gold wire. Distinct from everyone else in their drab, earth-toned, peasant Hebrew clothing. He comes into their waking vision. He appears tall, upright, aloof, yet totally focused. At a slow confident pace, he moves into the midst of the babbling crowd that jostle each other for the best view. They dare not get too close to him. He is the only person extended this respect. No one knows why. They sense a man of fearless regal proportions. Is he a messenger, an angel sent by our Holy Father, YeHoVaH?

One item of his apparel is obvious. The biggest, two-handed-sword, with the longest blade. Bigger than the Roman's biggest. In his belt it extends from his chest, showing off the ornate gold handle, against his black tunic. Eyes follow the long silvery gleaming blade that cuts into the earth at his feet as soon as he releases his pressure on the handle. Is he a warrior angel?

Statuesque, majestic, he focuses on the balcony of the praetorium. A bound, disheveled Yeshua on the balcony is his focus. Tears flow down his cheeks and disappear into his well-groomed silver beard. Thirty years ago, he carried gold, frankincense and myrrh to the baby Yeshua. A king of the east, one of the three Arab-Magi he stands still to witness the proceedings.

"Barabbas, Barabbas, Barabbas."

Pontius relents, motions to Centurion Antonius, the kindly Roman, one of the very few who has favor with the Hebrews. Pontius has a tone of impatience, mixed with a hint of growing concern about his own ability, and a tinge of self-doubt; hesitation.

Then he commands: "Bring Barabbas and The Rabbi here now!" The mob sees that the Prefect has made a gesture of some kind, and raises their combined volume to name the name that Pontius detests.

"Barabbas!"

Barabbas, the darkly handsome leader of The Sicarii (the dagger men) was caught and tried for murder of the Hebrew Elite. He justified his killings and claimed he killed only those who collaborated with Rome. When taken to prison Barabbas was lithe, strong and virile; outspoken, overconfident, rude and offensive. Imprisonment and punishment have reduced him to a thin, dirty, manacled, ragged, broken man. This is the image he now presents to the gathered Elite who once feared him.

His former enemies, the Hebrew Elite, think nothing of their own changing dispositions from concern about their own, who were murdered, to the more imminent threat from the popularity of the miracle worker, the Rabbi. The dangers presented by Barabbas and The Sicarii are diminished by the self-interest, economic and political control, which the Elite intend to keep.

Pontius knows legislative measures permit the Hebrew leaders to release anyone of their choice during Passover. He sees it as an example of their control over the system. (He fears this twist of legal manipulation will spin out of his control.) Ironically, his former prey - those prideful men - now look to Barabbas as a legal technicality they can use to manipulate the Prefect's attempt at justice. Now, the Prefect has been put into a position of political weakness, which may be strong enough to get him recalled to Rome unless he succumbs to their urgent, willful demands. With forceful hand movements, Pontius gestures to his men to direct the prisoners to the edge of the wall.

TWO YEARS BEFORE …

1
DEPARTURE

BEDROOM

Dominicus stands bare-skinned before a stoic Pontius. She pounds her small fists against his gold-painted leather breast plate. He does nothing to stop her. He takes what he deserves. She cries out, "You waited until the last day to tell me!?"

Pontius stands with thinning dark hair, physically fit, on the younger side of 'middle-age,' straightens his uniform to perfection, his preference for military attire rather than the flowing robes and togas of senators and princes. Until now dominating the conversation describing the people he is about to rule as "primitive." (Generalized, a superior Roman perspective of all the other people in the lands of their empire. They show Roman civilization through road building, and amphitheaters. His capability includes aqueducts.)

Dominicus, age 20 and mature beyond her years, tries to reach the smoky hemp of this man who burns reservedly with weighted quiet concern, like the warm, musky scented, candle sconces lighting the room. The heavy and oppressive fragrance in the windowless room brings her down sobbing at his feet. Pontius, torn by love for his wife and duty to his country, freezes in apoplexy, and searches his mind for something that will console Dominicus. She stands, throws herself back on the bed and climbs under the animal skins to seek comfort in their fur. Muffled, she asks, "You leave tomorrow?"

Quietly he answers her, "Tomorrow."

She regains her composure and asks, "Is Claudia going with you?" After a long silence, Dominicus's face and red rimmed eyes emerge from under the lambskin. Pontius nods to affirm his wife will travel with him to Judea.

She holds back tears as she rises and pulls on a robe and ties a rope around her waist. She stares intently and tries to think of a possible result for their actions.

"You'll be gone long."

She looks at him with the side-cocked expression of a temptress who tries to no longer care.

He ignores her so she adds, "Bother you?"

He looks down momentarily and then up at her.

"It does."

She moves around him to pick up the miniature figurine of Venus, the goddess of fertility. She waves it in his face.

"For this to work ..."

He interrupts her, "Superstitions."

"Claudia believes it!"

From his face to his lower abdomen, she thrusts it at him in frustration. He flinches. He takes it from her hand, and as he does so, she says in a state of controlled anger,

"It didn't work for me!" Frustrated, she thrusts her fists forward. He straightens his breast plate.

He could easily walk out but he does not. For his attention, she moves in close.

"So, the problem is you!"

She wants to slap him in the groin but refrains, barely.

"And Claudia will think it is her." She sniggers a breath of air, a snort. "How will you explain that?"

He places Venus in his tunic and puts a pouch of "chinking" coins down on her bed.
He walks to the exit and pulls back the curtain to let the natural light in.

She picks up the cloth tied pouch, throws it at him with all her might and watches as the coins spill, then ricochet off the walls. He glances back at her, pauses, then nods with compassion for her. He presses his lips together. Feeling torn, he leaves.

PONTIUS'S VILLA

In a near-by side street, two scrawny boys of uncertain parenthood, rummage along the edges in the hope of finding some stones and rocks to play with. Their faces show they are pre-pubescent (a mischievous age). These boys face a wall, adjust their garments and two individual streams of hot urine splash upward. One boy has rosacea on the right side of his face and aims higher than the other. The deformed pelvis of the other boy causes him to limp. Readjusting, shaking, being silly, comparing, they laugh at their own appendages.

They collect stones and uncover an iron rod, coated unevenly in lead, used in Roman construction to join building blocks together. This quiet residential street sits at a junction on a slightly elevated piece of land. From this position, the city of Rome may be viewed and approaches to the villa are visible on three sides. The small boys make a collection, piling the rocks to build a pyramid and amass ammunition for childlike warfare.

One says to the other, "The mouse lives here."

The other boy stares intently and compresses his lips from the side, raises his nose up and down, pulls back his ears so they flap backwards and forward, until his friend breaks his astonishment with laughter.

The boys are near a comfortable, modest Roman villa, the home of Pontius and his wife Claudia. This capital of an empire, opulent, busy, superior in design, civilized, on this fine day in 26 CE will be the last time Pontius will see it in this happy light. The next time he sees this city it will be darkened by the forces of injustice and the threat upon his life.

The physically fit Pontius, resplendent in his high-ranking uniform: An equestrian, he slowly rides through the streets on his magnificent horse. He seems content to put aside the thought of leaving Dominicus. An aura of restored confidence underpins his straight spine and his set jaw and square cheekbones. Confidence replaces compassion.

This day marks the end of an era and the beginning of change for him and his wife that will cause his name to become known throughout every future cathedral in the world. Until now he has lived an unremarkable life, climbing slowly up through the ranks. Nothing in his past, or the present, could possibly foretell his infamous future.

Pontius' friendship with the emperor Tiberius has no more solidarity than hearsay, no more substance than a glass of wine. Nevertheless, Caesar socializes with his advisors. The emperor prefers the solitude of the beautiful island of Capreae. He lives there, away from either real or imagined conspirators in relative privacy where he may indulge his fantasies. Some of the emperor's fantasies turn into fatalities. Pontius has visited there only briefly to accomplish business as fast as possible. Tiberius Caesar's slower pace, his island life, his penchant for a style of debauchery, depravity and utter cruelty, suits his semi-reclusive, not so secret, secrets. Of these facts Claudia Procula has knowledge, by way of gossip, not too far removed from the source.

Claudia's lineage, linked to Tiberius, but not clear by way of any family tree yet respected and admired. She won the attention of the emperor and assumed the honorary title of niece. For this reason and an act of pomposity, Tiberius will give Pontius and Claudia a royal send-off tomorrow on this rare occasion leaving his safe island for the dangers of the city. Good fortune protected Claudia from seduction and rape. Tiberius singled her out, but no one knows why, except she commands respect. Something he neglects - any respect of human life. Tiberius, a man of political cunning and double standards, is a murderer. Tiberius Caesar's former wife Julia, a rampantly promiscuous woman, still offends the Emperor. Hypocrisy of the highest order and his unimaginable acts of selfish gratification compound the warping of his mind. Julia, a total contrast to Claudia, who honors the security of marriage to Pontius with a sense of duty to the man and his new position; she possesses strength of will her husband admires.

Julia reports to Claudia the teenage nephew to the emperor, Gaius, a most unusual child, an annoying teenager and later on will be a threat to everyone he makes contact with. The son of the late Germanicus, a popular war hero, although precocious, arrogant and rebellious, Gaius gained the reluctant favor of his uncle Tiberius. Gaius also enamored the troops who dubbed him "Caligula," meaning "Little Boots," who as a child paraded himself around the camps in the apparel of a soldier. (As an adult, he will hate his nickname and behave in a manner even more depraved than his uncle Tiberius.)

Pontius's horse slowly approaches his villa. As if by instinct, his groom comes around the side of the building. In the distance he sees his master approach. The groom, a diminutive man, being the servant recommended by Julia and readily accepted into Pontius' and Claudia's private life. His name, Mus, Latin for mouse, a dwarf: Like a good wrangler, no coward when it comes to horses, he has an affinity with them. Neither horse nor mouse is able to speak. When the two small boys see Mus, their eyes dance with wicked delight.

Oblivious to the approach of the horseman, the boys pick up stones and hurl them toward Mus who skillfully ducks the incoming assault. Pontius, sees the attack, with a burst of good horsemanship, his heels to the flanks, approaches quickly and dismounts. Both Pontius and Mus join in the fun firing the stones back at the small boys. One of the boys hurls the iron rod through the air. At a foot-in-length, and unbalanced with the lead coat, it rotates through the air to fall short of the targets. Both Mus and Pontius consider returning the missile but seeing it could do damage, leave it on the ground. They continue to shower the boys with small rocks and dust. Overpowered by the barrage from Pontius and Mus, the boys turn to run off.

The boy with rosacea pulls the other who limps. They escape the barrage unharmed to look for more mischief elsewhere. Pontius picks up the iron rod, smiles at Mus nonchalantly, to take this potential weapon off the streets and enters the villa. Natural for Mus, no words are exchanged. The kind of satisfaction known only to comrades-in-arms, who have fought side-by-side, registers approval. His whiskers squiggle with delight as Mus leads the Prefect's splendid horse away for the night.

Claudia, a statuesque woman, leads Pontius by his arm through an archway. Evidently a happy household, warm smile, playful, she leads with a spring in her step as Pontius feigns to resist, waving the iron rod at her. "That rod will not make the baby," as she takes it from his hand and drops it on the fine mosaic floor. The dull thud of lead and iron cracks the fragile tile but they take no notice. She reaches into his tunic to retrieve the figurine of Venus and smiles with pleasure. She pulls him through the villa to their tiled sunken bath in the courtyard. Never for one tiny moment can he reveal he knows he is impotent. He will perform like a loving virile husband. He loves Claudia too much to reveal that he knows his inability to reproduce has been established by experimentation with Dominicus. Forced to conceal his inadequacy, he has no choice; he must keep the secret and subject his wife to reoccurring false hope.

ROMAN BARRACKS

Some distance away, in a barracks courtyard, three hundred soldiers, two cohorts, scurry hither and pile packing crates onto many horse-less carts. Centurion Lefus, tall, rugged, mean, and battle-scarred and the freshly handsome Centurion Antonius, an Adonis to many, stand nearby, supervising, counting the supplies.

PONTIUS'S VILLA

As night falls on the villa two guests arrive. An older couple greeted by Claudia. They embrace her and enter to join the already seated couple, older than the new arrivals. They sit with Pontius ready to enjoy a feast. Cousin Antonius arrives to take the only remaining vacant place. The conversation, not at all joyful as seemingly this farewell dinner party will be the last one for a long, indeterminate time.

The table ravaged, animal bones chewed bare and only the cores of once fresh fruits remain. Antonius stands to leave, cool, reaches over to kiss his cousin Claudia on the cheek to the acceptance of Pontius. Antonius says he will see them in the morning.

Pontius politely responds, "Good night cousin," although not directly related to him. "When we arrive in Judea, Antonius, I will not address you as 'cousin' you understand." Antonius nods, salutes fist to chest and leaves.

Claudia smiles as Antonius will be leaving Rome with them, good-byes are light. Not so for the visiting couples. Good-byes shall be tearful and wrench parents from their grown children.

To re-break the ice with optimism and excitement Pontius expounds, "Tiberius Caesar respects the Hebrew people."

At the far end of the Mediterranean Sea, the new Prefect of Judea and Samaria, anticipates his appointment with plans to bring civilization to the strange and primitive foreigners. He knows the Hebrew people are steeped in superstitions and rituals. Pontius pays little heed to the religions of Rome either, the worship of idols and gods. Ridiculous to Pontius, Claudia's figurine Venus, goddess of fertility, proof-positive that any religious practices and beliefs are futile, not effective. Yet he cannot disclose his secret affair. He understands the gods represent hope for Claudia, anxious to have their child. His affection for her precludes any admissions on his part. His pragmatism includes Roman engineering to consolidate his order and rule. He will be the one to bring two aqueducts to Jerusalem. His mission, he believes, brings with it an opportunity to gain favor with Tiberius for future promotions.

"We will keep the peace," with the intent to bring more civilization, plans to improve Judea as Pontius's dinner conversation within the family attempts to replace the gloom with the seriousness of his mission to the east.

"Agrippa's brother-in-law, Herod Antipas, is less known to me. We'll reside in his palaces."

Looking at their glumness Pontius refreshes their knowledge. "Emperor Tiberius knows well King Herod Agrippa, a frequent visitor to Rome. Hebrew independence came to an end eighty-nine years ago when we conquered Damascus and Jerusalem. The Roman Senate sixty-six years ago appointed Agrippa's father, Herod the Great, as King of Judea. Fifty-four years later, Tiberius succeeds Augustus." Pontius, aware of these political Hebrew connections, knows how Tiberius thinks.

Pontius hopes his personal attitude will inspire their parents to be uplifted, "A great opportunity for me to prove my worth to Tiberius."

Claudia pleasingly optimistic like her husband, playfully suggests, "Pontius the Peacemaker Prefect," while their parents remain sullen.

Pontius says confidently as he again raises his goblet of wine to all present. "Tiberius Caesar will be exceedingly pleased. I will bring prosperity to the people and fresh water to their happy lips,"

Claudia, however, puts her wine down, at the mention of the name, Tiberius Caesar. She looks on apprehensive; Tiberius causes her discomfort, since she was a child. The intuitiveness of youth has prepared her; memory courses within her veins.

"He is a man, for men, women, boys and girls. A festering scab. We escape Rome." She brings momentary silence to the room. Pontius' forehead furrows. Seeing the displeasure, she causes her husband she changes tempo again.

"My clever husband plans an aqueduct." She raises her wine this time.

"Fresh water for fertilization," Pontius explains with some whimsey in tone.

Claudia adds, "Cultivation for civilization." The statement underscores views Romans hold for the rest of the world. Wine has loosed their tongues. Claudia, like many, will generalize too. She will respect individuals, those who earn it.

She also reminds Pontius, "Antonius served in Judea. He made friends there. He understands their beliefs."

Pontius interjects with inebriated whimsy, "He's gone native!" And laughs lightly at his own joke, "ha-ha-ha!"

The evening draws to a reluctant close. The two older couples stand and divide: One couple to Pontius; the other couple to Claudia; they embrace respectively, teary eyed. One of the women gently rubs Claudia's stomach and looks her in the eye: Claudia shakes her head negatively. Excitement mixed with sadness for the young wife who longs to be a mother too. Their parents leave them to ponder the unknown.

Pontius takes hold of Claudia to catch her from the fall of emotion. His care for her, tinged with humor, "We will raise our son to be the Emperor of Rome." While most unlikely, he grasps for something positive to balance the secret that lingers within his conscience.

As so much keeps him mindful of his duties, they spend the late hours talking. Claudia asks the questions and

Pontius answers. He describes the challenges that lie ahead. The Roman Empire, a collar of land that grips the Mediterranean Sea and all the cultures and languages that reside there, has a neck hold on everyone. This outpost known as Judea and Samaria is occupied by a particularly intelligent and worshipful people. The Samaritans, despised by the Judeans, and vice versa, could become a contentious situation. Warned, the Prefect will be cognizant of this before departure. The land appears small and insignificant, but the people will present a contest. They have always resisted foreign invaders. Pontius's job as keeper of the peace will test his political skill. He hopes it will not employ military tactics also. His resources and recourses with might will be minimal. He takes with him only two cohorts of one-hundred and fifty men each.

As Pontius sleeps, Claudia busily packs her array of small figurines representing the gods that will help her through this new experience in the east. She wraps them in sack cloth placing them carefully in a basket. In particular, she takes the goddess of fertility, Venus, and presses it against her stomach with both hands, pausing for a moment, closing her eyes to imagine a small child. Unlike her husband, Claudia uses her will and faith in these gods to attract positive results. Pontius prefers to address that which he can see, touch and smell. Sleep that will refresh him presides over fanciful Roman whimsical gods and animal sacrifices that when cooked, merely feed the inner man with strength. Tomorrow he will need the latter.

2

PROCESSION

STREETS OF ROME 26 AD

The procession through the streets of Rome adds up to strength and a farewell exceeding the mission. Preparations for this journey to Judea, supervised by Centurions Antonius and Lefus, show perfect precision, they count everything. At daybreak, 300 Roman soldiers move purposefully to pack the last of the weapons, supplies, food and wine onto horse-drawn carts. Pontius, a minor power-monger, will govern Judea and Samaria, a minor province.

The ruler of Rome, Tiberius Caesar, has his own motive for the parade. He will view their departure as his own goodbye to the city. His unique administrative move to the island is understood by Tiberius, but to a lesser extent, those around him. An occupational hazard too, most Roman Caesars fear assassination. In his relative privacy, which is less accessible and safer, he may indulge his unspeakable practices.

Swelling the streets and eager with anticipation, Roman citizens gather on both sides of the road. The spring sunshine glistens on Pontius Pilate's highly polished head gear. In his chariot rides his wife Claudia and the groom, Mus, who must peer over the top of the handrail. Mus confidently holds the reins of two splendid grey horses. The crowd jubilantly returns the arm waving.

Ahead of them, Antonius and Lefus, ride abreast, on two black horses. They move at a marching pace. In front of them a small contingent of troops marches out of formation to spread the wide track in order to force the crowd apart, pushing them to the curb. Behind the lone chariot, more troops and two cohorts follow. At the back of the procession, all the horse-drawn carts pull the supplies for Judea and Samaria. The dust being kicked up gradually increases toward the end of the line: Out of this dust, a galloping lone horseman emerges.

The crowds cheer the lone rider. The fourteen-year-old relishes at any cost, the attention he can draw to himself. His outlandish costume hides his bandy legs; his cape flaps in the back draft; his ungainly hat falls off; he gallops on undeterred. The spectators behind him run to claim his bonnet. One of them dons the hat and does a silly walk to make fun of the future emperor. If it comes to pass, will he plunge Rome's notoriety down to the lowest sickening level?

Gaius takes a bearing on the range and the progression of the possession toward the reviewing stand. He calculates when Pontius's chariot should be parallel to the stand. He has it in his sights. He reaches Pontius, stops his horse, tears off his leggings to cast them aside. The crowd gasps as his balance falters. He then rides back toward the end of the procession pulling at his tunic. By the supply-carts, he stops, rips off his tunic and throws it at the crowd who scramble to claim it. Turning his horse, he rides for the front of the line, in a thin shirt and shorts getting ever more daring by standing on his horse. Knees bent, awkward, wobbling, his action has silenced the masses.

Tiberius Caesar, in the reviewing stand, peers at the approach of his nephew. Gaius rides dangerously across in front of the chariot. The crowd gasps. Mus eases the reins back to slow the chariot. The horses nay and jitter nervously. Down the opposite side of the procession Gaius generates cheers to detract from the main event, which is Pontius's departure. He looks at Claudia amused. Claudia, more reticent, shakes her head disapprovingly. Tiberius Caesar looks anxiously at this show-off; a spectacle of immaturity. He turns to an old friend, Senator Vinicianus, a battle-scarred, middle-aged man, surrounded by many of the members of the Roman Senate, raises his eyebrows as he is reluctant to say what he thinks.

Aside, Tiberius shakes his head,

"That boy steals our sanity."

Vinicianus nods in agreement and thinks to himself, *if Tiberius makes this boy his heir, which he may well do, the empire will be ruled by an exhibitionist fool.*

In the stand, at the peripheral distance away from these dignified men and women of Rome, one lady stands alone. Dominicus stares down upon Pontius.

Slowing and making the turn at the rear of the dusty procession, Gaius must sit down on his steed. On the return he puts his heels to the horse's flanks. Again, the horse speeds up to a gallop and again Gaius climbs to stand on top. The chariot, now abreast of the reviewing stand, and alongside the double-horse-drawn-chariot, he slows to a trot. Pontius looks apprehensive. His attention, drawn to the reviewing stand to glance up at Dominicus, and then down at Gaius Caligula.

Suddenly Gaius springs from his horse to land on the nearest grey horse. Startled, the horse rears but inhibited, twists the T-bar-section between the two chariot horses. The chariot begins to veer out of control as Mus fights with the reins. With nothing to hold onto, Gaius falls off the horse and onto the center bar barely grabbing it in time to keep him from going under the hooves of the horses. Mus pulls hard on the reins, trying to control the bucking horse restrained by the harnesses that attach them to the T-bar. One horse bucks while the other holds ground, they alternate, neither able to rear-up all their way.

The horses cannot rush off the way they want to, nor can they buck the trouble off their back and stomp on that unseen thing that unnerves them. Gaius tries to wrap his legs around the bar, but the horse is still thrashing, and the boy has not the athletic skills or strength he needs. Mus pulls the reins continuously until the horses stop. Pontius leaps over the handrail of the chariot to prevent Gaius from falling off the center bar. A few soldiers follow the chariot and move forward to investigate and protect the Prefect. Other soldiers break rank and crowd around the horse, several reach to grab parts of the harnesses to calm the horses. Mus has the horses under control. Pontius plucks the boy off the center section, holding the harness to steady himself. He reaches down, grabs the boy, and pulls him away from the possibility of getting kicked by the horses. He lifts him over the handrail and lowers him into the chariot with Claudia and Mus. Gaius, annoyed, shakes off Claudia's attempt to stabilize him.

"Leave me alone!" As he jumps down off the rear of the chariot to retrieve his horse. Pontius follows good natured and slowly.

The crowd has parted and Tiberius, with several Senators hastens to the accident. He looks annoyed at the boy. Tiberius acknowledges Pontius by saying,

"Gaius, the new Prefect of Judea saved your life. Thank him."

Hiding his embarrassed, unhurt, the arrogant, know-it all-teenager, blurts out.

"No, he didn't! He is a mere mortal! A man! I have a divine right to my life!"

Gaius grabs the reins of his horse. He callously slaps the sensitive mouth as if to blame the horse for his fall. Tiberius looks down at the boy, frowning. Tiberius shakes his head sadly and says.

"Nevertheless."

His horse tries to pull free while Gaius remounts. Caligula aggressively points to Pontius,

"The gods Mercury and Jupiter used him!"

Good-natured, forgivingly, Pontius laughs toward the boy.

"You may believe whatever you like Gaius Caligula."

(Gaius detests the nickname "Caligula," the name meaning "Little Boots" given to him by the troops when he was a small boy when his mother dressed him in the costume of a soldier.)

Pontius, a man of practical and liberal beliefs does not follow Roman religious ritual. He allows Claudia that indulgence.

He leans closely to Claudia, "I did not feel used or pushed in that foray."

Suddenly Dominicus appears standing next to the chariot. Momentarily Pontius freezes in fear of what Dominicus might say to Claudia.

Gaius viciously digs his heels into the flanks of his horse and gallops away from the procession, his horse neighing and baying objections at the youth. Tiberius faces Pontius. A silent thank you, a sign of respect, a traditional Roman salute, Pontius raises his fist to his chest. Tiberius and the others turn back towards the reviewing stand. Dominicus remains observant, next to the chariot, raising anxiety in Pontius. She stares. Claudia notices them both and says nothing.

As Caligula rides away, Claudia, always in search of a little whimsy to humor her husband, nods towards the retreating boy.

"Little Boots. Big clumsy feet."

She puts her hand gently on Mus's shoulder. He turns to smile. Pontius steps up into his chariot and also smiles. He presses his mouth to her ear and whispers, "We don't want a son like him."

Mus nods. Claudia waves. The crowd cheers. All the while Antonius and Lefus have remained spectators from on horseback and now turn to move off at a walking pace.

Tiberius returns to the stands to view the procession as the soldiers get into their lines. He knows his nephew will need education if he is to rule the empire one day. Pontius waves at the dignitaries in the stand but Dominicus has already disappeared.

CAPREAE

On the island of Capreae, Tiberius Caesar settles into his luxurious bad habits. Secluded, he is free to indulge his fantasies. Far from being an attractive man, in his late-sixties, his oval face is pock-marked; his thinning gray hair just about covers his spherical cranium. He moves his glistening robe to scratch and expose his bandaged legs. Lounging back in happy contentment he stares at one of the boys. Several well-groomed young boys and girls sit around, bored, somewhat lost, perhaps drugged or hung-over from too much wine. The size of Caesar's stomach displays the ample good life he enjoys. Fresh fruits lay all about him. He languishes until his eyes lasciviously lock onto a pretty young boy at the edge of the group. He beckons him forth. The young boy shyly approaches. Tiberius pats the pillows next to him and gestures for him to sit. As soon as the boy sits, Tiberius puts his arm around him.

"Do you know how to wrestle?"

Terror shows on the boy's face; he pulls free quickly and runs away. As he flees, he does not see Gaius Caligula hiding behind a marble column. The formerly embarrassed horseman, now still, is tall, unattractive with a broad forehead, hollow eyes, pale skin, wispy hair, thin legs, and big feet. He lurks in the shadows like a spy. Just out of Tiberius' line-of-sight, the voyeur looks on.

Victims aplenty, Tiberius reaches for a young girl who sits near him. Without resistance from her he puts his arm around her tiny waist and marvels how petite she is and takes her hand to measure her muscles. He smiles the smile of someone sick with predatory perversions. The little children look away.

Caligula slips away into the shadows to teach the runaway boy a much-needed lesson about submission to Caesar. No one denies the ruler of Rome anything he desires.

(Private tuition will give Gaius a command of languages, the arts, and military tactics. From his uncle he will learn to be suspicious, jealous and at times, callous and inhuman.)

3

OCCUPIED LAND

JERUSALEM

The Temple in Jerusalem dominates a high point of land that overlooks the city below. Ranked next to the Temple, two other buildings hold claim to architectural prominence. The Antonia Fortress, the Roman barracks, the courtyard, sits high and while less mighty than the Temple; it thrives with comings and goings. Next to the Temple, not too far distant, King Herod Antipas's city palace, houses Pontius Pilate, Claudia and the entire household, when the procurator needs to be in town. The other palace, quite large, located within the city walls, appears to be preferred by Antipas.

A crowd made up of individuals who wear simple earth tone garments in contrast to the brightly clothed Roman citizens, quietly exit the Temple together. In this peaceful crowd, a nobleman wearing fine fabrics, decorated with tassels and gilded ropes, makes his way to divide the retreating congregation. Those in lesser attire recognize stature and step aside to allow him free passage. A group of non-participant young men, on the crowd's periphery, huddle together, and whisper among themselves: Their line-of-sight focuses on the nobleman.

The young men follow their leader, Barabbas, a tall, darkly handsome man, about thirty-five, fit and strong. He now places his hand under his shabby garment. Judged by his clothing alone, he lives rough in the same clothes every day.

His beard is unkempt and does not totally hide his high cheek bones and steely look. The young group moves in through the masses to mingle and depart with the flow of direction.

Barabbas maneuvers alongside the nobleman who looks sideways at him: Getting closer, Barabbas covertly takes his hand from under his garment, expeditiously with a great thrust, forces his dagger to enter below the rib cage and upward into the heart; the nobleman groans, eyes-wide-open, and falls to the ground, dead.

Barabbas holds onto his knife, which now drips with blood. Without even wiping it he conceals it under his garment. The young dagger-men known as The Sicarii, have succeeded to obscure the vision of those around them and they surround Barabbas to hurriedly leave. Individuals in the crowd fall back. Some stop and stare in disbelief as blood weeps from the fallen nobleman to stain the dry earth.

The Sicarii, known by reputation, hide in the hills. Ambush and murder with zealous indignation all those they consider treasonous. They believe the Judean citizens who collaborate with Rome, should be eliminated to liberate their country. To take back that which the God of Israel had given them.

4

GRAVEN IMAGES

JERUSALEM

The instruments of war are lined up against a wall: Curved wood frames, canvas straps and leather shields, stacked up ready for distribution. A few artisans sit around sewing twine through leather. Another paints the profile of a face; another, an eagle. These craftsmen and womenfolk occupy a workshop where their toil continues unnoticed. (Perhaps not for long, soon these heraldic Roman shields will be the talk of all Jerusalem, but they will not be the true instruments of peace.)

THE FORTRESS

Inside the courtyard of the Antonia Fortress, Roman soldiers stand atop ladders to fix the shields high up and out of reach. They have not considered one wall faces the Temple and may be clearly seen by the worshippers. This has not been considered by the Prefect or anyone else. The profile image, although a poor likeness of Tiberius, represents a mark of respect that Pontius has commissioned to ingratiate himself with Caesar. The illustration of a bird of prey reminds everyone that the eagle rules the sky and the earth, or more accurately in this case, Rome has conquered this earth. The soldiers busy themselves at night to avoid the work in the heat of the day.

A young boy snoops, watches and waits. Seeing a vacant ladder, he makes sure none of the soldiers pay attention; he scales it quickly and tugs at the shield until it breaks away and crashes to the ground. Aroused by the noise of falling shield and stone, the soldiers approach the ladder: The boy descends into the obvious trap; they are amused by his struggle. They make the mistake of using him as sport, pushing and shoving him around, deriding him in the language of Rome which he does not understand. The playful beating entertains them, but they do not realize he has a good kick and fast legs. The boy's right foot hits the nearest soldier in the crotch and brings down the mighty hero in an instant. The boy breaks free, runs for the exit, out through the gate and into the darkness. The soldiers can only be amused and laugh at the misfortune of the other.

At dawn, a group of noble Hebrew leaders stand aghast at the display of shields in the barrack's courtyard. Shaking their heads, pointing out the perspective, the Temple is in sight of a fully decorated wall, one shield after the next in a horizontal row. Never have they been so insulted by their rulers who promised their customs, traditions and religions would be honored for the sake of peace. Never have they had to make this kind of complaint. Does this new Prefect not know how grievously he has insulted their God of Israel? He must be called to remove the heathen, graven images of gentile worship. They plan to report Pontius to The Chief Priest, Caiaphas. They know Caiaphas will be displeased; he is a man who will not let anything go until agreement with him is reached; a man who thinks himself beyond reproach.

CAESAREA MARITTIMA

At Herod's sumptuous seaside palace in Caesarea Marittima in Judea, Pontius and Claudia relax on the terrace overlooking an azure blue Mediterranean Sea that stretches out of sight, calm, breathtaking. They sip wine. This could be the perfect romantic setting where they might conceive an heir. Caesarea boasts a fine amphitheater for horse racing. This hippodrome will provide the stage for a boastful horseman known to many. Interrupting the idyllic atmosphere, a forced cough announces an arrival. Centurion Lefus enters, clearing his throat.

"The Temple High Priest and his Jewish Council, from Jerusalem, to see you." Pontius not pleased, is taken by surprise. Claudia walks to a small display of idols to pick up a figurine of the Roman god Mercury; she thinks the same thoughts as her husband and expresses them.

"They have come to see you which will save us a journey to Jerusalem." She turns apprehension into hope.

Pontius looks at the figurine in her hand, "They probably stink after two days on those donkeys." "That" – pointing at her idol – "I doubt will bring us profit."

Pontius and Claudia follow Lefus out of the room, taking their wine goblets with them. As they go out the doorway, Claudia turns to Pontius and smiles.

"They will need your aqueduct."

He jibes, "In Jerusalem, not here."

The entrance hall is a large room with a high ceiling and fabric covered walls. Large open windows reveal a view of landscape on one side and the Mediterranean on the other. The late afternoon sun settles into the west. Pontius and Claudia stop a short way into the room. Lefus proceeds to the entrance, outside which the delegation waits.

Lefus leads an older man, still physically fit, and a group of eleven others. The Jewish Council of Elders stop in front of Pontius at a respectful distance: Lefus indicates the leader and formerly introduces them. Pontius, unaware of their mission begins with a smile.

"Greetings from Tiberius Caesar."

Pontius seats himself in the only chair set to the side. Claudia steps back and stands at his shoulder. Caiaphas looks at her in a silent, disapproving glare, thinking this is no business for a woman.

"My wife, Claudia, great niece of the emperor."

Claudia smiles her most beguiling smile at Caiaphas but unable to befriend the Chief Priest she glances down at her husband who waits for the first utterances to come from the group before him. The Prefect knows the simple psychology of control. The person seated and the one who does not speak, he holds the power to hold onto his throne.

Caiaphas, who has had two days of travel to think about his opening statement, now hesitates. While utterly determined to have his own way in this matter, he faces a new unknown leader from Rome. He will put the Prefect in his rightful place, a mere gentile, a conqueror, nothing more than a bully, a thief who tries to steal not just their land but the land given to them by their God of Israel, their YeHoVaH. So sacred is the name YeHoVaH, these devout men utter this holy name respectfully and sparingly. Caiaphas feels beneath himself having to make a request, a suggestion, no, a command of this damnable Roman intruder. All this anguish and at the same time a need to preserve their economic base, he attempts a little charm too. It does not last.

"You will not make any graven image for yourself, any carving, and any likeness of anything." [Exodus 20:4]

Claudia looks again to the figure of Mercury in her hand. She wonders if this little object of idolatry in her hand is the carving Caiaphas refers to; *how odd,* she thinks.

The words fall upon Pontius's ear, but don't penetrate within. However, he must, while quietly seated, mentally digest the possibilities of this communication. Grappling with the knowledge of four languages he concludes it sounds somewhat formal. Pontius in his attempt to keep the proceedings on a light level replies,

"Caiaphas, some refreshments after your journey ..."

With the first signs of this man's impatience Caiaphas blurts, "Those shields must be removed."

Pontius looks at Caiaphas with some realization and adds, "What images have you seen?"

Caiaphas takes a step towards Pontius. "Those shields which you have put on the walls of the Antonia Fortress, in front of our Temple! They must be removed at once."

Pontius smiles, "To honor Caesar."

Caiaphas cuts in and repeats, "They must be removed! At once!"

Pontius raises his eyebrows at Caiaphas; snaps his fingers, makes hand signals to Lefus in the shape of a bowl of fruit. Lefus leaves to find the servant girl, Shira. The Prefect makes it plain.

"Your position as High Priest is a debt to Tiberius Caesar."

Caiaphas, frustrated, continues, "This is a sin against our YeHoVaH who forbids the worship and adulation of such despicable things, this idolatry of yours!"

Pontius, calling upon his own pomposity, lectures the High Priest, "Caesar, in his benevolence toward you and your people has upheld his promise to respect your beliefs, your religions, and your superstitions. Without reservations, Caesar has extended to you these extraordinary concessions, unlike anywhere else in the Empire, because he respects your agreement to a peace between us, whereby *you* enjoy *our* protection. Therefore, the standards are a symbol of our promise to keep that peace and I assure you; Caesar will be well pleased with them."

Pausing, Caiaphas, in an awkward silence, stares down the Prefect in defiance.

The beguiling Hebrew servant girl, Shira, appears with a bowl of fruit to distribute to the silent delegation. Shira focuses on Caiaphas. Lefus looks to consume Shira. Pontius does his best to continue smiling and thinking aloud, "You prosper from Caesar's benevolence, so honor this," to gently remind the High Priest that his livelihood depends upon Rome's tolerance. Pontius attempts to keep a more ingratiating tone of less aggression.

Lefus' constant looks at Shira cause her to ignore him. Caiaphas shakes his head negatively at Shira to refuse the fruit. He looks to the Council to do the same. Some have already taken of it. They hold it in hand not allowing their hunger to be satisfied. He burst forth, "Tiberius Caesar will *not* be pleased" Caiaphas thus begins his threat.

Pontius thinks clearly despite the wine, still able to control his exacerbation, hammers his point again, and repeats, "You enjoy your wealth thanks to Caesar." Somewhat incredulous he finds Caiaphas fails to acknowledge the privileges he enjoys.

Caiaphas grows more agitated, cuts in yet again. "Prefect, I must caution you. These images offer no protection; these shields are a direct insult! In full view of our Temple! They are not a symbol of God; they are the symbols of heathens, devil-worshipers and gentiles. You will agree to have them removed now or we will take alternative steps to have them removed."

Pontius has heard the covert threat plainly, but he tries again to find even one, reasonable bone in this obnoxious man. "Marc Anthony was the protector of your king. Your king built the Antonia Fortress in his honor and in Marc Anthony's name. As indeed this same king, your king, built this palace. I am here, appointed by Caesar Tiberius, to protect you, your people, and maintain the peace."

The High Priest stands aloof on a firm plain level like one about to spring a silent and swift attack. The snake slithers down but his tongue quivers with venom, "Prefect, you underestimate the seriousness of your offence against us. I can assure you Caesar Tiberius will be displeased with *you*."

Pontius pushes up from his chair. Rising to his feet he unwittingly concedes to a contest with his standing opponent. Caiaphas holds his ground and increases his cloaked threat.

"Prefect, you misjudge us."

Not so well concealed Pontius barks, "What? You dare to caution me?"

Pontius shouts at the group, "We protect you!"

The Jewish Council shifts, uneasily. When Shira approaches the members of the council, they return the fruit whole or half eaten. Caiaphas barely under control; his rage seethes below the surface. "My people are assassinated!"

Pontius shouts, "By your own people!" He signals Shira with his empty wine goblet to bring him more wine. He breathes deeply. Caiaphas pushes home his point.

"Those images are a direct insult to my people and our God YeHoVaH, our God of Israel, our Elohim who gave this land to us!" Caiaphas, adamant, puffs and sighs, flexing his emotional outbursts with righteous authority. "And you took it from us!"

Pontius pauses, considers his response tensely, and then gets in close. In his face with quiet intensity, he tells

Caiaphas, "You trifle with me here." The Prefect has no time for a god he cannot see. Claudia remains standing by her husband's empty chair. Her fingers turn the figurine she still holds.

Caiaphas matches his demeanor. This first interview, a contest of wills apparent to all and doomed to fail. Neither contestant has created room to step down or to save face. "Have the shields removed now! Or we will take countermeasures," he blurts.

Shira returns with a wine skin to top-up his goblet. Pontius turns from Caiaphas and appeals directly to the Hebrew Council, "I assure you Caesar will be well pleased with this recognition, this honor, this sign of respect." Shira hurries out of the arena looked upon closely by Lefus who has not the least interest in the proceedings and the most interest in her receding.

Pontius holds his hands out in supplication. Appealing to them he suggests that this demonstration of their dislike for the shields will have an opposite effect: To keep the peace they should not contest the shields. Removal does not honor Tiberius and does not show any gratitude they should have for their ruler who has bestowed wealth and power upon them. He continues his lecture to keep their existence harmonious and friendly, they should acknowledge their ruler Tiberius. Pontius, flabbergasted that he is about to lose this argument, walks up to individuals in the Hebrew Council and directs his statements to each of them. Looking from one face to the next, he searches for an ally: He finds no friends in the group: He suggests they not be controlled by their overbearing leader. "Stop. Take a vote."

They argue in circles with Pontius, that the shields may be seen from the Temple. To face west the heraldry looks down upon the east side. The Temple for their God and their people, the laws of their Almighty God are all insulted by this display. The presence of these pagan images, these false gods, these shields is an abomination to YeHoVaH. The meeting turns to bedlam as one speaks upon another. The Council prefers to seek the approval of Caiaphas, Pontius notices.

Caiaphas tries to regain control of the argument. "Prefect…" He motions to his group to settle and they do.

Impatient now, Pontius cuts him off. "Cohabitation requires cooperation!"

No responses from the council, they are mute, under the influence of their leader.

Antonius enters having heard the raised voices, curious to see the Hebrew Council all of whom remain silent now except for Caiaphas. Standing quietly to the side, Antonius automatically puts his hand on the handle of his sword.

Pontius glances at Antonius, to conclude matters, defeated, he nods, "Antonius, escort them out."

Pontius turns toward Claudia, holds out his arm to the one he can depend upon. She steps forward, places her hand on his wrist and they turn their backs on the room. They leave Caiaphas and company as a clear signal that the Prefect has no intention of submitting to their demands. They are Caesar's subjects and they will respect the authority of Roman rule.

On the terrace, without saying a word, Pontius and Claudia, she sips, he gulps his wine. She faces an angry, very red-faced, Pontius. His coloring made even darker by the reflection of the setting sun. She knows about timing, to give him a few moments to collect his thoughts. The sight of the blue sea that reflects the darkening blue sky may absorb some of the blue air as the sun settles in the west. She hopes this calm weather will console him. The first meeting with a group of significant individuals important to the stability of the political climate has caused a little storm. She looks down at the figure of Mercury in her hand, and then she smiles.

"This god of trade and commerce is of no help."

"That presumptuous, arrogant, vain, blackmailing, single-minded, High Priest…" Pontius looks at the figurine and glances back towards the Entrance Room.

Pontius shakes his head to dissipate the anger.

To break the tension Claudia laughs teasingly. "You don't like him, do you? So, stay here with me. I can improve your mood." Pontius smiles, and with a sigh of relief takes Claudia into his arms. The embrace reminds him of the comfort that this woman he loves and respects provides. Dominicus is now far out of his mind. Claudia intends they should enjoy the seaside and the horse racing at the Hippodrome nearby.

Caiaphas, the Israelite Council, stunned, remains outside for a moment. The sun sets on the beauty of the sea and darkness falls. The Chief Priest rises from defeat, "The people will do what I tell them to do. The Prefect has yet to learn who possesses the real power in this land."

5

SIT DOWN

ON THE ROAD TO JERUSALEM

The sounds of horses' hooves pound the earth. Romans on horses. Farmers work the land, till the soil, spring gives rise to hope. The Romans on horseback turn them into by-standers. They look up as the conquerors from Rome press on; a moderate yet imposing uniformed force.

Pontius Pilate, Centurions Antonius and Lefus, with a half-a-dozen soldiers canter along the dusty road from Caesarea to Jerusalem. This day's journey need be no more than a minor show of some aloof Roman pomp. They reach the Antonia Fortress just before nightfall.

(Vastly different groups from the warm personal reception that will greet Yeshua as He processes into Jerusalem, a peaceful convergence yet to take place in the days to come.)

THE ANTONIA FORTRESS

The next day the fortress is alive with troops who go about their routine and have become accustomed to the curiosity aroused by the shields displayed on the walls for all to see. They accept this peaceable perusal, the Prefect's homage to Tiberius.

Pontius waits for Caiaphas and company to surrender to the harsh sun, and the still oppressive heat, to bring them down weakened from thirst and hunger. There are no breezes within the walls of the fortress.

After a brief and general inspection of this display to honor Tiberius, Pontius stops to ponder his actions. He knows Claudia does not approve of Tiberius. Now all the residents of Jerusalem demonstrate their disgust. So, what is he likely to gain, he wonders? If this demonstrates his thanks to Tiberius for his appointment to Judea and Samaria, Pontius has made a political mistake that could escalate. He tries to think of something he could say to those who sit quietly. Knowing they are under the spell of Caiaphas he reserves his actions and strength.

Pontius walks into the fortress with Antonius and Lefus. In an administrative room, a table displays a model of architectural designs and closer inspection draws the Prefect closer to a structure that might resemble a bridge, but it is in fact an aqueduct. He sits himself and addresses the two men who await his command with a switch of his frustrations.

"We did not come here to let Caiaphas have his way. Find the leader of The Sicarii, Barabbas! I don't care how!" He pauses and smiles, "ALIVE is preferred!" He has not lost his sense of humor but changes tone again, "Search, contact, arrest!" The Centurions glance at one another. Pontius dismisses them with an impatient gesture. He wonders, *will this deflect the unfavorable interest in the shields and force the Chief Priest to be an ally?* (The next six days will be dogged and bogged in stalemate. The tenacity of the Israelites deadlocks with the stubbornness of The Prefect.)

The Centurions and a contingent leave hurriedly. They know exactly who Pontius refers to; Barabbas, the murderer who slays the Hebrew Elite. The mounted Romans startle those seated. In particular Lefus who rides threateningly close to scare them. Antonius rides away from them. The Roman detachment rides out of the city toward the hills.

Antonius has gained the respect of some Hebrew leaders. His gentle manner is approachable. Comfortable, they read him as easy to work with. The kinder of the two Centurions, the cousin of Claudia and therefore a social link to the man at the top. They know direct approaches could lock them into a forced agreement with the power of the Prefect. The leaders work their connections wisely to take control. (Antonius, reputedly generous, gives to their temple treasury. No one really knows why but the political implications may be sound reason or perhaps more likely his senses have the conscience of a Hebrew.)

After they depart, Caiaphas, followed by a large group, and Annas, and the Hebrew Council, all solemnly file into the courtyard of the fortress. They sit down near the wall and the mounted shields. While they find their back-less seats uncomfortable, their rigid straightened backs show pride and determination. The soldiers look on mystified. To satisfy the curiosity of the few amused soldiers, Annas, the eldest of the group, points out the shields. He shakes his head disapprovingly and the Romans find the encounter nonthreatening. Annas pulls a light-colored fabric over his head to protect himself from the harsh sun. The soldiers wander ominously around the passive, seated, elders to monitor them. One Roman makes haste to The Prefect.

Unexpectedly, Claudia and Shira enter the courtyard mounted on the same horse. Their escorts, two Roman cavalry guards follow them. The horses flutter and jitter after their long journey. The soldiers come to aid the new arrivals and take hold of the reins. Claudia dismounts, sees the Chief Priest, his group seated about him and the shields on the walls. A soldier directs Claudia and Shira across the courtyard to the main building, a stairway to the administrative room.

Absorbed with the architectural model, Pontius raises his head when he hears female voices approach. To the soldier who waits for a reaction to his report about the sit down, Pontius merely says, "Leave them alone for now." He turns and to his surprise, sees Claudia, who is all smiles in hopes to beguile him. Shira, apprehensive, stands back while Claudia embraces him.

"That was dangerous" he says with reference to the journey.

"I brought Shira" she said, making light of his concern.

"Adding another prize for the bandits" he says with a mixture of alarm and an understanding of his wife's plucky nature.

She changes topics. "The Chief Priest sits down in the courtyard?"

With sarcasm, "Our friends, who came to see us in Caesarea; I come here to investigate the murders; the men the Sicarii envy. And those who sit down there because my shields offend their God? Can you understand their priorities?" Pontius suggests they retire to Herod's palace in the city, where they will reside in safety and comfort.

THE STREETS OF JERUSALEM

He instructs four soldiers to accompany them, two ahead, two behind: a boxed march. They carry shields for protection. This walk will redirect the tired legs that sat upon horses all day. The Prefect and his entourage do not see someone in the periphery who shadows their leisurely stroll. The warm streets are busy. The silent boy creeps along and takes cover behind other people. The bystanders see him acting suspiciously and shove him off. The citizens who see the Roman contingent, fall silent in their presence. The shadowy figure emerges from behind a donkey. He runs to a bend in the street still unseen by the six strolling Romans and their servant Shira who hides her face with her thin shawl. Over the cloth her eyes stare in the direction of the boy. The very same boy who climbed the ladder and threw one shield to the ground appears empowered by his own perceived invincibility. His daring reaches a peak.

The boy darts out from behind a building support, looks into Shira's eyes, and rips the shawl from her face as she screams. He runs for all his might into the back streets pursued by the two rear-guard soldiers. Pontius instantly turns around, views Shira, and the back of his two soldiers. Immediately at the top of his voice he screams the order, "Re-form, re-turn!" Pontius knows that such an incident could be a distraction for an ambush.

The two men return, "We could have caught him."

Somewhat disturbed by their lack of forethought, he says, "That boy could be a decoy. Never leave your post when in my presence. Your duty to protect these women exceeds the importance of that boy's arrest." The four soldiers with shields re-form the corners of a box around Pontius and the two women. They march in a tighter group.

Shira, still shaken, is surprised she was singled out; the only Israelite within the six Romans. Claudia explains, "There's a group of men, barbarian murderers, who will think your service to us is treasonous."

Shira considers her response to her mistress. "A special man, his name is Yeshua, I heard he ..." The friendship between the servant and her mistress has to be consolidated but not yet.

Suddenly and shockingly the sound of loud cries come. "Ahhh" and a group of six near-black Arab bandits emerge and rush the five Roman men. The Arabs mouths are open, their cloaks flap, and they attempt to gulp in their success to blanket the Romans. Claudia grabs Shira and pulls her in tight with extraordinary swiftness of thought and action so they are back-to-back in the middle of five men. Pontius already has his sword unsheathed. They form a tight box but with gaps between the shields. The attackers have identified the Prefect and try to break through the defenses.

Pontius turns side-on without the benefit of a shield. He uses the same tactics to thrust out at the assailants. His protected position between two of his men who could close the gap between the shields if he would back down and squeeze in with Claudia and Shira. Pontius continues to thrust his sword between the gaps. He makes a piercing contact and the injured man staggers backwards. The four soldiers lower their shields to slash over the tops at the approaching Arab swords.

Claudia, in the middle of the shielded human box, jammed against a soldier, sees a knife in his belt. She seizes it, aims and flings it toward an attacker with the aplomb of a knife thrower. Beginner's luck, it hits a shoulder and the Arab drops his sword. He retreats. Suddenly the others lose their will. Their war cries are reduced to whimpering as they withdrawal. In a moment they are all gone. The streets are barren. Only the hot settling dust remains. The Romans keep their formation until they are absolutely sure the danger has gone.

The quiet hush is broken by Claudia.

"Phew. The day of a long ride, a long walk and a long throw."

"I married you for your skills with a weapon."

Shira shakes, so highly strung that Claudia firmly hugs her.

They cautiously march on in a defensive formation. The soldiers about-face at the palace once Claudia, Shira and Pontius enter. Mus holds his hands in the air when he sees the ladies to let them know there's nothing wrong with his ears, just his tongue. Pontius tells Mus they left their horses at the fortress. The groom shakes his head. Pontius knows it is safer on horseback as was just proven.

ANTONIA FORTRESS

The next day Antonius and Lefus, who are dirty and tired, face Pontius. They have been out all night in search of the Sicarii without success. Shyly, Antonius suggests the shields that face the Temple might be removed, which may reduce some of the objections. Antonius respects the Hebrews and is sympathetic to their wishes. Pontius listens.

Lefus, adamant, counters the idea as ridiculous. "Put *more* shields up!"

Pontius appears to be too passive for Lefus. He says with calculated reasoning, "They will want to quench their thirst; they will go home soon."

Lefus looks at his men and smirks a little. "These old men are of little concern. But, the leader of the Sicarii is."

Antonius accepts both the lightness of his statement and the heaviness of their failing to find Barabbas. Inside Lefus lurks an aggressor, the military solution, to use might and force against the weak protesters, destroy and conquer them. He does not understand diplomacy, he understands fear.

His patience waning, Pontius asks Antonius and Lefus, "Barabbas?"

An alarmed soldier interrupts to bring news of the situation. "The numbers increase. They quietly remain seated."

The Prefect decides to hasten to see for himself. The centurions hurry behind him.

Pontius paces the top of the wall, displeased with Lefus and Antonius. "Did I, or did I not, make clear, search, contact, arrest? Where is Barabbas? Is he in that mob?" Both Centurions shake their heads from side-to-side. Scanning all the men seated in the courtyard, he asks again, "Where is Barabbas?" Pontius hopes the arrest of Barabbas will go some way to appease these Hebrew leaders.

"We were in the hills," Lefus' voice reaches a higher pitch. "Antonius gave up." The familial connection Pontius has with Antonius makes for a less than formal relationship. Lefus senses this.

Pontius knows they are very different personalities. He had hoped they would complement one another. Instead, they compete. Lefus has also seen Shira catch glimpses of Antonius and has a suspicion she is interested in him.

The Prefect has time on his hands to decide what to do with the seated Hebrews. For now, he remains passive, taking a-wait-and-see approach to the problem. "We will starve them out," he says.

Lefus, with insubordination, says, "They hide food in their garments, this will not be effective."

The Prefect will hold his order for force while his patience may last. His patience with Lefus has a term limit.

Antonius returns to his room in the barracks, which is in disarray, with weapons piled up, and garments and uniforms on the floor. Tremors quiver through a boy's paralyzed body. He leans over his boy servant who lies on the hard ground.

Antonius picks him up and places him on the bunk. He shows greater concern than most would show.

THE COURTYARD

At night the seated men get up in twos and threes, leave, and are quietly replaced by others. Antonius walks, little hindered by the growing crowd. He draws near to two well-dressed Pharisees: The Noblemen, Nicodemus, and Joseph of Arimathea. He walks to them, drawn to their appearances. The change of watch overseen by Nicodemus and Joseph, both mature men display the apparels of success and good standing.

Others around them sit down. Antonius enters into a quiet discussion with them. "I need a physician to help my servant." A small number of Elders approach the three men standing. Nicodemus and Joseph hesitate to make assessments of this Roman who stands boldly before them. The Elders, more familiar with this Roman, listen. Antonius asks, "How do you heal your people, do you have a physician?"

Nicodemus explains that their obedience to the law promises them good health: "The Laws of YeHoVaH." Detached and about to ignore Antonius, Joseph adds,
"Romans have pagan gods and idols, Roman priests and healers, sacrifices, drinkers of animal blood, so why should he not ask *them* for *their* help. Why ask us?"

The Elders stand around, look kindly toward Antonius, nod their agreement, this is a solution for the gentiles. They also know this Roman of Greek origin has paid respect by contributions to the Temple taxes. This therefore allows the Elders to treat him differently.

Antonius says, "My servant is an Israelite." In the faded light, Nicodemus moves in more closely and then recognition strikes him. Joseph adds his acknowledgement.

Joseph says, "Ahhh, I know of you."

Nicodemus plunges with excitement into a story. He tells Antonius that there is a Rabbi in Capernaum who heals the sick. There may be an opportunity for him to take his servant there. One of the Elders speaks to Joseph who then adds, "For he loveth our nation." (Luke 7. 5.) "You have a good report among all the nations of the Jews."

In the distance, Centurion Lefus looks around, scans them, to see most of the mob seated, some doze peacefully. While Antonius appears to be surrounded by those who stand: This causes Lefus to approach quickly. He hopes his colleague may be involved in something contentious so he can draw blood. "Antonius? What's wrong?"

"Nothing." Antonius has no desire to open up the conversation with Lefus present. He leaves the group. They look blankly at Lefus. This allows their perceptive minds to reason this man Lefus intrudes. Their Centurion friend walks away: The one with dangerous eyes follows, curious about his colleague.

Under the hot sun, the next day, the mob, a greater number, sit quietly. Some Roman soldiers walk around in perplexed amazement that no action is being taken. The orders are to leave the seated mob alone; the soldiers question the leniency of their leader. Among themselves the soldiers talk about their training and exercise space being taken. "He does nothing." They know to brandish their swords will quickly disperse these unarmed men who are no counter force to a Roman army.

They look up to see Pontius who walks the top of the wall alone. He takes in the view. The soldiers wonder what he is waiting for. He descends the stairs from the wall. Walks across the courtyard: The soldiers become alert expecting his command. Instead, he enters the stables and takes his horse. Mounts, rides out slowly, and pays no heed to the groups of hot and thirsty men seated around the courtyard. They are trained to kill or be killed. The soldiers look, see him go, to leave them impotent.

THE PALACE

He rides the streets of Jerusalem without apparent concern for his safety. The previous ambush has not intimidated him. Pontius has more courage than his men will credit him. The horse has a presence among donkeys and the people step aside to allow him to pass. The palace entrance is guarded and monitored. The faithful Mus takes his horse from him and Pontius enters the cool stone building.

Shira straightens the bed furnishings while Claudia combs her hair listening. "Remember. When we were attacked. I was going to tell you about a special man Yeshua. I was told he has done great things for our people. His name means 'to save.' He is a Rabbi who knows all the history of our people, he performs miracles."

When Pontius reaches the bed chamber, he finds Shira and Claudia. Claudia knows what could be on his mind. She turns to Shira and asks her if she knows anyone in the crowd at the fortress. Shira says, "I know a few in Jerusalem. My home is Bethany."

"That mob tests our patience" Pontius mumbles under his breath. "More so my men than me. I could wait them out until their clothes rot off their stinking bodies and they become bored with the constant routine to change places with one another."

Claudia swings around. "You said they would get tired and thirsty, but will they?"

Pontius knows it, thinks it and says it, *"They are clever."* They have strength and a deep desire for independence rooted in their belief in their God, YeHoVaH. He knows he has a very difficult task, "Patriotism, difficult to quash, especially when irrefutably linked to a belief in something much higher than man himself." Pontius knows it will be near impossible for him to break the adhesion that is invisible to the human eye, but he will try.

Claudia looks at Shira, silently warns her with wide-eyed expressions she is about to sling a few words at her husband for fun. *"Cleverer than you?"* Pontius looks at Claudia wryly, shakes his head, turns, grunts and leaves. Claudia cunningly smiles at Shira and quietly says to her. "He really loves a challenge." Shira could never take such chances with the master of the palace.

THE ANTONIA FORTRESS

As day slinks into night Antonius leans over his Boy Servant with a bowl of gruel. His quarters cool while his concern warms up. He exits into the barracks courtyard to anxiously walk around the groups of seated Hebrews. As some Israelites newly arrive, others depart. Relief is smooth, quiet and swift. Some soldiers wander the periphery accustomed to the gatherings of human obstruction.

As Antonius approaches an Elder, he stands up to recognize him. Antonius stops. "It has been days now." He refers to the deadly sickness his servant suffers, not the tediousness of this sit-down, stand-off, an objection to the shields. "Ask the Rabbi to heal my servant."

The Elder feels the stares of the curious soldiers and nods positively at Antonius, who leaves quickly, glad to have a mission and somewhere to go, with something important to do. Not everyone thinks or does what The Chief Priest expects. They are a minority, but rumors travel. The Elder will now journey to see the miracle worker. This Elder has been told, the man of mystical mystery, speaks with authority. This Rabbi preaches something different than the Temple where their leaders expound on the Oral Law. This teacher mingles with the common people. He speaks with kindness. He describes another realm, another place of habitation, a place where no earthly concern is relevant but where true peace resides. This Elder will find out what is the truth, what are the lies, and can the Rabbi perform this miracle of healing for the Roman and his humble servant?

THE PALACE

Herod's palace buzzes with a small party but with nothing yet to celebrate. Pontius knows the importance of social unity to gain professional progress. He entertains his highest-ranking officers; Centurions Lefus and Antonius. They lack the rank of a Tribune who would be there with a larger force; a legion, some one thousand to six thousand men. Jerusalem's small number of armed men, Pontius thinks, will need to be increased to maintain the defense of the land and the people.

Shira enters with fresh fruits and more wine. Lefus has a good look at the servant woman. He knows the dangers of seducing or raping someone so close to Claudia. Anything he might attempt, any advances upon Shira will be reported. Lefus resents the limitations he has had to apply to his own life within this circle. Shira secretly admires Antonius but could not possibly become involved romantically with a gentile. Shira senses when Lefus stares at her and she must force herself not to look so admiringly at Antonius for fear that Lefus will notice. Neither Roman nor Israelite could reconcile to each other. Shira knows Antonius, a kindly man, who has a mystifying respect for many Hebrew people, very unlike most Romans. Shira stands to the side to serve and quietly observe. This is all she is allowed to do. She must deny her intuition.

Pontius announces that he awaits the arrival of the "Ingeniare." Rather than risk the misuse of the instruments, the dioptra, an astronomical surveyor's tool, and the chorobates, enabling levels to be found, these complicated measuring devices must wait for the man who can use them proficiently. Blank faced, Lefus and Antonius await their orders. Pontius stands, paces, stops, looks into their blank faces to see blank minds. "Instruments! You can't use them. The 'Ingeniare' he will need them. For the aqueduct."

He has another job that they are more capable of, if they will just apply themselves. "Find the Sicarii." The men become restless to leave, energized with a little wine to give them false courage. Claudia stands to listen. The Prefect plays with them. "Bring them all in. You failed to bring me Barabbas last time now bring him and *all* of them."

"They hide in the hills and then ambush," Antonius dares to say.

"Tell me something I do not know." With hand gestures he shoos them off. They leave, sensing his impatience.

Claudia takes her husband by the hand and leads him back to a lounge area. He then playfully pulls her onto his lap. She reminds him, "Horse racing by the sea; you promised." He kisses her gently, a complimentary kiss, and thinks about it but knows they cannot.
She knows what is on his mind. "That mob has been there on the ground for six days." Claudia, dismayed, kisses him gently on the lips. He stirs, quietly turns angry, his face glows purple. Finally, he concludes very slowly, he will have to exercise his rank with the force and the rule of Rome.

6

FOREGIVENESS & HEALING

Elevated above the masses, the bowmen on top of the fortress wall surround the courtyard square, stand at ease and wait. On the periphery of the square, at ground level, heads turn slowly, while soldiers on alert, wait for their orders. Mus obediently holds Pontius's horse; The Prefect scans the hard paved square to view the seated mob. The silence loudly proclaims extreme tension exists between military power on alert and passive resistance in decline.

The very large and docile crowd seated on the ground while Pontius inwardly marvels at their fortitude. He has never seen such defiance at this quiet, very still level. A man underrated, cast upon this far corner of the empire, considered a minor player in the politics of Rome. Called upon to be an administrator, tax collector, military leader, instigator of civil engineering works, magistrate, keeper of law and order, he could never anticipate this peaceful protest. He eyes his men on top of the wall itching and twitching to load arrows into their bows and show off their marksmanship. The courtyard could soon, very easily, with no effort or real skill, become a lagoon of dark red blood.

Pontius looks to his servant, Mus and subtly shakes his head from side to side, then mounts his horse. He looks to his Bowmen and signals them to load their bows. Like the bellows of a beast in a quarry that echoes, his voice carries around the walls.

"Take aim!"

Each Bowman holds the arrow tensely, refrains from fully extending it, at the ready and prepared to fire. The crowd, one-by-one, stands up in fearful anticipation, an ominous murmur of movement. Pontius, alone on horseback, weaves between the ever-quiet, nervous crowd. They look up at him on his horse in an unspeakable, heart-pounding, unbelievable, paralyzed state of dread at this definitive moment. Their imminent deaths lock them together, they huddle. Their adherence to the laws of their God of Israel, creates an atmosphere so pungent, the air becomes putrid as some bowels let go.

Pontius shouts at them, "Clear the square!" His agitated horse, clip-clops, nervously as it absorbs the tension. The Prefect sits firmly, confident he has the total power to take life, or grant it, as a stay of execution. He comes upon Caiaphas. He stops abruptly. The Chief Priest has influence over his people that Pontius cannot comprehend. Why would all these men sacrifice their lives for this display of artwork and at this repugnant unpleasant man's radical insistence? The Prefect brings his horse close to Caiaphas. He peers into the eyes. At the top of his lungs bursts forth again, "Clear the square!"

Defiant, Caiaphas remains silent. The stand-off, the contest of wills, the extra ordinary reserve that Pontius shows, the competition between his impulse and his patient restraint, a quality of experience. Takes practice from the battlefield to know when to hold back, when to advance, when to strike. He again attempts, by a threat, to move these men out of the square by gentle persuasion and mounting frustration.

"This is your last chance!" he broadcasts at short range to Caiaphas but for all to hear.

A long tense moment; Pontius's horse faces Caiaphas. He looks around at his bowmen to see their concentration directed at the masses. He becomes vulnerable in their midst. Any of the bowmen who miss their target could easily wound Pontius. Nevertheless, he sees the need for a tight string of intimidation which when slackened, will release injury, death and chaos, perhaps a stampede. He leans over the mane of the horse to get so close to Caiaphas that his spittle sprays him. "You can leave now. Peacefully: Or see your own blood spill before you."

Like immovable rock, without a flinch of any feeling, Caiaphas ignores him. Pontius waits. The Prefect now has time to think through some theater as if they were in a hippodrome. A circus requires more than one act.

"Antonius! Come!"

The Centurion hastens on foot to Pontius's side with soldiers behind him. No side-show; the man with top billing goes first.

"Start with him!" He points at Caiaphas. At long last Caiaphas expresses an inner fear.

Centurion Antonius hesitates as Caiaphas responds, "We keep the law; Our God comes to our aide!" he says this with his fists directed to the heavens. His next statement challenges Pontius and calls his bluff, and attempts to demean his authority as trivial.

"We prefer death to disobedience!"

The challenge accepted; Pontius Pilate initiates his staging. "Take him for all to see!" Using hand signals to move the troublemaker to the middle. Antonius directs his men to grab Caiaphas and drag him to the center of the square.

Caiaphas, forever insubordinate, shakes and struggles to make the soldiers tighten their grip. "Emperor Tiberius told you to honor our customs! Remove these shields."

Pontius follows on horseback. Incensed, at his mention of the Roman ruler, pulls his sword from his scabbard and raises it skyward using it to motion his soldiers who stand around the square at ground level, to tighten upon the group. To make clear, he adds, "Close in. Reduce your range to your sword's length!"

Uncooperative, The Chief Priest, slips, loses his foothold, forcing the soldiers to drag him unceremoniously. Desperate yet articulate, he says, "You can pull us by our hair, but we will return until you remove those abominations to our God of Israel."

Pontius remains on horseback approaches Caiaphas.

The soldiers form a circle to contain the mob. He nudges his horse forward, leaning in again. "Get your people out or they will see you executed on this spot."

Pontius directs Centurion Antonius to put Caiaphas down on his knees. Antonius fumbles with Caiaphas who resists. His reticence noted, Lefus moves Antonius aside;

rough-handles Caiaphas to his knees, pulls his upper torso forward to push him face down and roughly pulls back his garments to expose his neck for execution.

Caiaphas, in a strained voice says, "Take down all the shields and I will disperse my people."

Pontius points his sword at the condemned and states, "I'm not here to negotiate with you. You are in revolt against Caesar."

He looks around and motions with his sword to direct his bowmen. "Stand at the ready." Caiaphas trembles. Pontius studies the old man then looks around and makes an announcement, "I will spare all those who leave." He waits for movement but there is none. "Take aim!"

Some bowmen intermingle with the swordsmen to tighten the group. They point their arrows at the nearest victim in the mob. Some of the youngest men in the crowd wet their garments again and shake with fear. The bowmen perspire in the heat of the day.

Pontius rises up on his stirrups, "Move out now. All who remain will be cut down!"

Caiaphas speaks to the ground. "It is far better to die than be a slave to Rome." The idiocy of this remark does not escape Pontius. The tension will snap when the first bow string releases its deadly arrow.

Two well-dressed noblemen, Nicodemus and Joseph of Arimathea, rush forward waving to gain Pontius's attention and they do. Joseph pleads, "Sir, our law commands us. They have no choice."

Nicodemus adds, "Our laws are the laws of our Almighty. But you have a choice."

Joseph in haste keeps up, "Your laws are made by man."

He hears the voices, tries to look around, Caiaphas says, "You remove the shields and I will remove my people."

Silence reigns. Pontius looks up at the shields and then incredulously at Caiaphas. He looks around at the soldiers who perspire under the hot sun, poised ready to slay the tightly formed mob, circled with bows, fingers and taught strings that shake. Swords at the ready to thrust forward sparkle in searing, mirror-like flashes, hands that seek blood. Lefus holds his sword eager to remove the Chief Priest's head from his shoulders.

The wait is an intended torment: All eyes are on Pontius.

"My final order" He looks down at a defiant Caiaphas and says in a moderate tone, "Your people must leave now." Frustrated, he pulls hard on the reins of his horse so the animal circles. He walks the horse and limits the chance of the horse kicking one or more of his men. Mus, on alert, approaches the horse. His men stand back. The horse rears. All those in the vicinity immediately move back. A magnificent animal of regal strength. The stallion is controlled by Mus, who holds the harness, and rubs the neck briskly. Pontius remains mounted. The soldiers sweat. The tightly compressed crowd trembles in the heat, soaked in perspiration. The horse shakes his head from side to side. He dislikes his confinement. Suddenly, Pontius motions to Antonius, unexpectedly.

"Remove those shields which face the temple." Pontius re-sheathes his sword, nods toward the bowmen, and lowers his hand vertically. "Stand down!" He motions Lefus and the soldiers to sheath their swords. Antonius sighs with relief. Lefus's jaw drops in shocked wonder and total disappointment. The Prefect directs his attention to Antonius and points to the shields that face the Temple.

"Assign those men. Get the ladders. Remove that row!"

Victorious, Caiaphas stands up and beckons his people to follow.
Caiaphas hastens, "Come, let us depart this place." And he pushes them along. To wait a moment longer could cause the Romans to change their minds.

Lefus thinks the Prefect too weak for his command. Pontius knows his thoughts. Lefus wants to engage. Tuned to be aggressive, he gets the direct order from the Prefect. "Keep them moving. Use hands and feet only!" Rebellious, Lefus can only huff and puff.

Pontius looks at his servant, the horse wrangler; Mus. Pontius turns his horse around to face the throngs of departing people. He has won the day militarily, diplomatically and civilly. Some of those who depart even acknowledge him for it. They respectfully smile relief or wave at him. Those few, who do so, make sure Caiaphas does not see them.

And to Centurion Lefus, "We will show them mercy. Allow them to leave unharmed." He hopes that will be a lesson to him. A trained wild animal should be kept in a cage.

Unseen by Pontius, Lefus turns, nods, inwardly disapproves, repeats the order to the men closest to him and with hand gestures. He does a little frivolous shoving, tries to capture some successes for himself out of what he believes to be defeat. To other soldiers more distant, Pontius shouts, "Withdraw!" Lefus picks up the word and relays it with apathy. The troops stand down.

Nicodemus and Joseph have heard the word, walk against the drain of their people as they flow out around them like rocks in a stream. They catch the eye of the rider. Mus slowly brings Pontius's horse to them. Victorious; he leans over the mane to get closer to Joseph and Nicodemus who also witness the removal of the shields in progress.

"Your Caiaphas would sacrifice men of raw courage. For them, not for your high-minded Chief Priest, I do this."

They nod thankfully and leave. Slowly the mob disperses. Mus holds the reins. Pontius observes the crowd moving away peacefully, many of whom regard Caiaphas the wise winner, his demands met, and respect maintained.

The minority who have the good sense to acknowledge Pontius gratefully leave with their lives. Merciful and forgiving as Pontius has been this day, even fewer will give him any honor or respect. They cannot argue with the brute force. They have yet to see the Prefect instill more fear. Their obedience to his will, when it comes to his passion for fresh water, that will come.

THE PALACE

Pontius relaxes with Claudia, "Why did you let them go?"

"Because I believed their devotion." The strain of the day has tired him. He knows fanaticism may be misguided. He explains to Claudia. He gave them recognition and consideration because their protest was a peaceful obstruction. He hopes he has won their favor by peaceful means.

CAPERNAUM 27 CE

The Sea of Galilee provides the fishing grounds for the people of this small town on the north side of the shore. Agriculturally, Capernaum, also known for the nearby oil and grain mills, helps to sustain one synagogue. A humble, soft-spoken man, of extraordinary knowledge and talents, captures the attention of the townsfolk. He speaks with quiet, calm authority, and recites the Torah; word perfect. He soon gains their respect. His name in Hebrew, Yeshua, means "to save." This common name does very little to underscore or emphasize his growing reputation as a miracle worker.

Nevertheless, word has travelled; this Rabbi is young and popular with the ordinary people.

The broad back of Yeshua, face unseen, obscures the eager faces of a small audience. The Elders from Jerusalem anxiously approach Yeshua with a specific request. One of them boldly approaches him with confident expectation. "Rabbi. A worthy Roman, who loves our nation, has a tormented servant who lies paralyzed." [Luke 7: 2, 3, 4.] This man serenely examines the new arrivals who stand before him: He takes moments to study each one of the Elders, looks into their eyes, one wonders if he reads their thoughts.

"I will come and heal him," [Matthew 8:7] He says with simple acknowledgment and a belief in their needs. The Elder tells Yeshua where he may find Antonius and his servant.

THE ANTONIA FORTRESS

The Antonia Fortress in Jerusalem, now devoid of the offending shields considered pagan and disrespectful by the Israeli Elite, has returned the square to normalcy. The excitable Elder, who has good news for Antonius, scurries.

In his centurion's quarters, the grey, skinny, near-death boy servant lies prone, twitching. Antonius stands by as the Elder enters and bubbles forth with an announcement: "Yeshua comes." And the Elder leans in to take a closer look at the boy.

Antonius says with concern, "No, no, not here! Tell Him I am not worthy that he should even enter under my roof." (Luke 7.6)

The entourage of onlookers listens to Antonius. "But ask Him to only speak one word, and my servant will be healed." (Matthew 8.8) The Elder looks upon Antonius somewhat bewildered. A conversation ensues.

CAESAREA MARITTIMA

Herod's Place at Caesarea lit with candles, a relaxed Pontius sips from a beaker of wine. Claudia places her collection of small figurines within a shrine, and an array of smaller burning candles. Curiously she continues her conversation. She refers to rumors and stories, the source of which is not known. Shira attends to their needs, with wine and food, in a casual manner.

"A miracle worker, a Hebrew, a Rabbi," Claudia announces, to get the attention of her husband. He looks out, scans the ocean that surrounds the three sides of the palace. He stops to think about what Claudia has stated.

"Crazy hearsay. Until you see the proof." Pontius says because he has heard such things before. He has been told about the soothsayers who use their claimed expertise to take advantage of the gullible. To make a living, to earn money, has more to do with commerce than an uncanny ability to foretell the future. The Prefect looks whimsically to Shira, thinks she may well be the source of this false sorcery.

"My informant has my trust." Claudia jibes, "Or more importantly, your trust."

"The Prefect's wife has informants?" He mocks her for amusement.

Claudia enjoys the banter. "Surely, as your wife, if you have my ears, I can be your ears too?"

He stands next to her. "So, this miracle worker. He is a magician?"

Claudia clarifies the definitions, "A magician plays tricks, but a miracle worker heals the sick."

He moves around, looks out to sea. "Claudia; Mythical beliefs: Superstitions." He looks at Shira raising his goblet. She tops up his wine while having knowledge of this subject, but she refrains from adding to their discussion. A listener may glean far more than the speaker, and she knows not to speak until spoken to. He looks to the mature servant with a smile, knows she would have information that Claudia will have extracted from her.

He ponders the testimony, looks to Shira for a reaction: "Your informant, given *her* predisposition to myths, tricks, soothsayers, misplaced beliefs, is not reliable. It is not proof." But Shira gives nothing away.

Claudia notes the word "her" – Pontius has made an incorrect assumption. "My informant is neither Hebrew nor woman." He walks to her shrine. Shira leaves. He looks to the small figurines; the idols of the pagans.

ON THE ROAD IN JUDEA

The sun shines from Capernaum to Jerusalem, a small group stands around Yeshua. The Elders stand in front of Yeshua. Their conversation appears expectant. They are uplifted with hope. The one who has become their spokesperson explains the Roman Antonius to Yeshua with an ardent admiration for both men. Antonius "… is also a man under authority, with soldiers under him. He says to one 'Go' and he goes. To another, 'Come' and he comes. To my servant 'Do this' and he does it." [Matt. 8:9 Luke 7:8] The Elder hesitates and then with more seriousness, "He asks you: 'say one word and his servant will be healed.'" [Luke 7:7]

Yeshua considers what he has been told about this Roman who has a servant who suffers in a near-death state of hunger, dehydration, shaking yet paralyzed, slowly losing his life. Yeshua turns to the small group.

"I have not found such great faith, not even in Israel."
[Luke 7:9]

THE ANTONIA FORTRESS

In the barracks, the boy servant, healthy, sits eating as the Elders enter. The miracle of this healing is complete. They marvel at the proof.

CAESAREA MARITTIMA

Simultaneously Claudia conveys to her husband the news leak of this miracle which has travelled fast from Jerusalem to the seaside palace in a day. Pontius stands, looks thoughtfully at Claudia who insists, "The very instant, at the Rabbi's command."

"You are very taken in by this fable." He paces. He picks up the small figure of Mercury. "For Antonius, ridicule, unless he attributes the trick to this." He shakes the figurine at her. "In this country magicians and pick-pockets outnumber the servants and their masters. Antonius must say it was the gods Jupiter, Mercury, who saved his servant. Claudia, don't say it was the Rabbi." He puts the figurine back down. "In the eyes of his men, this will lower their respect for him. Do not heed this miracle worker!" Pontius looks out at the ocean. Her silent hushed thoughts anger her. Claudia snatches Mercury from him. She moves to the little shrine of Roman gods. He calls to her, "Superstitions run amok." He wonders what she plans.

She gathers the figurines, Jupiter, and the rest of them. Hurriedly Claudia walks to the veranda overlooking the cliffs and hurls all the paraphernalia as far as possible into the sea below: Pontius speechless, shakes his head and chuckles in amused disbelief at his wife.

7
PLOT

Sunday, October 12, 27 CE
[The Chronological Gospels, Michael John Rood, Page 161]

JERUSALEM

The Elite assembly consisted of the usual power mongers eager to conspire in the chilling still night air as autumn sets in. Appearing before Caiaphas, the Pharisees and Sadducees, together with Annas, Caiaphas's father-in-law, they fix their eyes on the Temple Officers. Anyone who disagrees with them will find the temperature drop.

"Why have you not brought him?" [John 7:45] asks one of the Pharisees who refers to the arrest of Yeshua Ha Mashiach. The Officers, stand sheepishly, then counter, defensively.

"No man has ever spoken like this man!" [John 7:45] One officer says, and Joseph of Arimathea listens intently.

A Pharisee counters with a contempt for their ignorance. "Are you also deceived? Have any of the rulers or the Pharisees believed in him?" [John 7:47, 48]

The Temple Officers, under the employ of these men are reluctant to offer a defense for Yeshua.

The Pharisee again, pompous, proud, refers to the ordinary rural people who live a lackadaisical existence.

"These people who do not follow our spoken Torah, our Laws, are all cursed." [John 7:49]

Nicodemus shifts on the spot and picks up the legal argument. "Does the Torah allow any man to be judged before he is heard and before diligent inquiry is made into the accusations?" [John 7:51] Joseph of Arimathea looks at Nicodemus and with pursed lips holds his ground and confirms with a nod.

"Are you also from Galilee? Search as you may you will see no prophet arises out of Galilee," [John 7:52] the Pharisee exclaims Yeshua is not from Galilee but from Bethlehem. Caiaphas and Annas exchange a look; an impasse; an agreement in silence. Everyone left the meeting. With no arrest the issue remained unresolved.

To hold onto their political power, the Pharisees, would have stoned Yeshua to death if they had the chance. The Sadducees would be more inclined to use their political influence and collaboration with the Romans but the opportunity was yet to present itself. Not satisfied, heretofore unable to gain the advantage over Yeshua, they reconvened again one cold winter evening.

Early March, 28 CE

Caiaphas, the Pharisees and therefore the Sanhedrin, stand in an intense debate. A witness from Bethany testifies, "Yeshua cried out 'Lazarus, come forth' the dead came forth. I saw it! I believed him." [John 11:43]

The Sadducees, who do not believe in resurrection, began to talk among themselves to disrupt the assembly. Caiaphas, with the power of his position, prevails upon them, claps his hands together to quiet the group. He has the Sadducees within his agreement, so he turns his attentions to the objectors.

Caiaphas puts forth the simple question: "What shall we do?" [John 11:47] As a snake will rear up and backwards before striking his victim.

An Elder objects and says defending Yeshua, "This man does many miracles!" [John 11:47]

Caiaphas walks directly to this Elder threateningly, "If we leave him alone, everyone will believe in him." [John 11:48] The High Priest swings around to hear support before he strikes.

"And the Romans will come and take away both our positions and our nation." [John 11:48]

Caiaphas looks pointedly at the dissenting elder and shows his fangs, "You know nothing at all." [John 11:49]

Then looks at the Pharisee. "Nor have you considered that it is expedient that one man should die for the people." [John 11:50] Venom drips from his mouth. "Rather than the whole nation perish!" [John 11:50] His eyes and his rotating body scan the gathering. (From that day forward, they conspire together because they are determined to put Yeshua to death. [John 11:53]) Caiaphas slithers away.

76

8
COMPETITION

CAESAREA MARITTIMA

The large oval track surrounded by high stone banks bustles with spectators who surround the hippodrome and the periphery. They are there to see King Herod Antipas. He journeys to Caesarea to be an uninvited guest in his own palace. Pontius and Claudia, *not* thrilled to share his palace with him, make the most of it. The crowds anticipate the formal arrival, a small contingent, a caravan of camels. Antipas lounges in a sedan chair carried by eight physically fit slaves with dark sunburnt skin. No doubt this is more comfortable than a camel.

Antipas, a political strategist, militarily timid, personally insecure, always surrounded by his Palace Guards, has brought his wife Herodias and her daughter Salome, his niece, with him. Salome has the scruples of a debased, conscience-less, predatory animal with cunningly lethal tactics.

Previously, during an evening of celebration, the evening of Antipas's birthday, Salome danced so provocatively for him and so pleased was he that he promises her, in the form of an oath, anything she asked. Her mother, Herodias, told Salome to ask for the head of the prisoner John the Immerser, as he is known in Hebrew. Antipas, distraught, recognized John as a holy man, a man whom he could respect, someone who had given him good instruction, but Antipas rejected it. John the Baptist, as he is better known, told Antipas that it was unlawful to take his brother's wife as his own. He really wanted to execute him, but for fear that John's supporters who believed him to be a prophet would cause a revolt, he bound him in prison. Now, in front of his peers, Antipas made a promise and was forced to exercise his oath to save face with those gathered. He commanded the execution and the head of John, delivered to Salome on a silver salver as she requested but it did not give him any satisfaction. She then gave the head to her mother.

John's disciples took his body for burial and informed Yeshua.

Antipas proudly proceeds around the hippodrome racetrack. In tandem, in a separate lounge of a sedan, wife and niece-step-daughter flop along behind him under a canopy; their bearers are fat, an indication their testicles have been removed to make them impotent and therefore no threat to seduction or rape. The eunuchs guard the womenfolk with more blubber than bravery. The menagerie of entourage creates a theater unworthy of respect.

Pontius prefers a separation so he may maintain a quiet command over the noisy false exuberance of the tetrarch. The Prefect and Claudia remain modestly grouped with a few Roman soldiers in the stone terraces. Antipas would make friends with the reluctant Prefect who prefers to remain distant.

As per this occasion, Gaius Caligula, now twenty years old, makes an entrance behind the small procession of camels and sedan chairs carried by slaves. Gaius displays a repugnant and gaudy costume. His intent to intimidate looks hideous. Herod, Herodias and Salome all jostle along, wave to the spectators. This display has an air of circus about it. Tiberius's nephew adds something clownish.

Gaius postures, his fine horse prancing up to the last camel. Gaius, prematurely balding, tall and lean, big feet, stands on his saddle, shows off his horsemanship, rides along the side of the sedan chair. Antipas, highly amused, waves Gaius on enthusiastically. He is unaware that Pontius knows this could end in disaster as it nearly did in Rome if he had not saved Gaius from being trampled to death. The tetrarch plays up to the nephew of Tiberius to win his favor. His political hand so obvious it embarrasses Pontius.

The Prefect turns to Claudia quietly. "Look how the puppeteer plays his puppet. The string-puller *from* Rome, Gaius. The other, the puppet *of* Rome, Antipas". Pontius suspects the puppeteer might be in-line to pull all the strings of Rome. Antipas allows his strings to be pulled. He wants to make sure his friendship with Gaius is maintained. Antipas acts like a sycophant.

Gaius prances around the track intent upon being the main attraction. He sits on the back of his horse, releases the reins and bobs from side to side on the rump. Herod Antipas makes his way to the stone terraces upon which a wooden stand shades the king and his immediate entourage. The king's Palace Guards form around the box. The camels are led away with the empty sedan chairs and horses and their riders take their positions at the starting line. Gaius pushes forward on his horse, takes the reins and trots until the marshal waves his arms at Gaius to get into formation.

Antipas looks toward The Prefect for recognition, but Pontius keeps his line-of-sight on the horses. They are about to start the race. The flag raises then swiftly lowers and the horses and riders leave a cloud of dust as they pass the cheering crowds. In the raised enclosure, King Herod Antipas, Herodias, Salome, and the king's palace guards, all look to the race. Pontius and Claudia sit a short distance away: A snub.

Gaius lags behind the second horse in third position. As much as he tries, his horse will not pull forward. He tries to make his horse nudge and bite the rump of the horse ahead but fails.

A poor loser, he pulls up the reins of his horse, and stops midfield as the others swerve around him. King Herod Antipas looks amused, quizzical. He anticipates some shenanigans. Pontius shakes his head in disbelief.

Gaius lets his horse trot as he watches the race progress around the other side of the hippodrome. As the racehorses complete the lap and catch up to Gaius' position, he digs his heels in, making his horse gallop ahead of the pack. Gaius keeps his horse ahead, weaves, and prevents the real leaders from overtaking him. The flag drops behind Gaius thereby to pronounce the second horse as the true winner. Gaius, however, rides on, accepts the crowd's boos, hisses, and arm waving. The attention he craves even when delivered negatively he accepts as triumphal. Kneeling on the back of his horse he takes his victory lap.

Antipas looks again at Pontius: They make contact. The Prefect rolls his eyes. Their posturing for power becomes somewhat impotent. Pontius has relaxed, his tension gone, but only momentarily.

Being from a different culture and class, Pontius has a natural enmity for Antipas. He inherited his position from his father King Herod the Great, while Pontius had to work hard to gain respect and his promotion. Born into wealth, Antipas has lived the easy life, secured by the Emperor of Rome. Born into an equestrian middle-class, Pontius, proven to be self-made, driven by ambition. The Prefect has little interest in this lazy faux king, this pretender. Their common moment passes.

Antipas sends an emissary to Pontius to invite him to his party. How can he refuse? He lives in Herod's seaside palace! Antipas makes the assumption that his invitation will be seen as a polite gesture. He knows that Tiberius has briefed Pontius about the favor he has to extend to the part-Hebrew, part-Arab, King of Judea.

THE PALACE BY THE SEA

Pontius and Claudia, now peculiar hosts to Antipas, while Antipas, plays host to the Prefect. The dualities of hosts make uncomfortable bedfellows. Vying for social prominence, Antipas is loud while Pontius and his wife remain conspicuously quiet. Antipas, with extra guests, Palace Guards Herodias, Salome and Gaius Caligula, will draw Pontius to him if he can. He wants to be friends with Pontius who has been able to avoid him until now. Painful to watch, awkward, Antipas tries another tactic.

Antipas singles out the young man from Rome, "You were not the fastest today, Gaius." Expecting Pontius to further his opinions, The Prefect remains stoic. Gaius and Pontius have mutual disrespect for one another.

"The one who comes in first is rightful in his claim for a prize." Gaius looks admiringly at one of the beautiful servant girls Herodias has brought from Jerusalem. His statement,

Gaius knows, laced with ambiguity, made clear by his ugly stare at the girl. Will others in the room see his lecherousness? The servant girl looks away. Antipas continues his struggle to make this a good party. All the trimmings of food and drink are present, but the atmosphere lacks good taste.

"Gaius you cannot win a race with words." Antipas says.

Herodias and Salome take an interest in Gaius and his stare at the servant girl. Pontius, as yet not even acknowledged by Gaius, decides it is time for him to make himself known: To remind Gaius of the time he fell off his horse into the Prefect's chariot.

"I am sure his horse has the right words for him!"

The assembled group smiles, although unlikely they will know the real undercurrent of his reference to the accident in which Gaius could have been seriously injured had it not been for Pontius's intervention. To overcome the awkward tension, Gaius expresses it with hysteria, drawing more attention to himself by imitating the neighing of a horse.

He gazes toward Pontius then turns inward and retaliates. "The Prefect of Judea thinks his own skills as a horseman greater than mine."

Pontius refuses to be drawn into a petty argument with a young man who retains a dangerous child within. Salome sees an opportunity to draw the real Gaius back onto the stage. He blatantly cheats in the hippodrome. She wants to see if he will equally entitle himself to anything he wants whether it be a horse race or racy behavior.

"Gaius. We have seen your skills with a horse." She beckons the beautiful servant girl to come to her. Eyes downcast, she gets nervously closer. "What would you do with this girl?" Gaius has spent many an hour with his Uncle Tiberius on the island of Capreae. The private atrocities Caesar Tiberius committed give license to his nephew. Claudia visibly shakes and shudders with the knowledge she has.

Gaius takes the servant girl's hands, pulls her forward, down to the marble floor, so she is on her hands and knees. He pushes her bottom down, then all four limbs down. Like a horse, he climbs over her and sits on her back. Claudia knows the ways of the debauched Uncle Tiberius, his role model. They all laugh, except Pontius and Claudia, who leave in haste. Mounted on the servant girl, Gaius Caligula watches as they leave. Herod Antipas, Herodias and Salome find some relief as they see the source of their tension has gone. The Prefect has again avoided a social entanglement with the fun-loving, frivolous king, the detached, ineffective representative of his Judean people. At last Herod Antipas and his entourage left for Jerusalem.

EIN GEDI

Claudia and Pontius relax under the shade of elaborate canopies, ornate tents and enjoy fresh fruits with other Roman couples. Near the seashore at Ein Gedi, a beautiful oasis is made more idyllic by the absence of the young Gaius Caligula. Claudia predicts they have not seen the last of Caligula. She sees the precocious boy as an influence upon his uncle Tiberius Caesar. Claudia also knows that Tiberius must name an heir and will straddle the line to name joint heirs and include Gaius's brother Gemanus.

A lone horse and rider appear. Closer, recognized as Roman, not an Arab. The soldier dismounts, perspiring, tired; he approaches Pontius, simultaneously intercepted by Lefus. Pontius looks expectant.

The cavalryman, identifiable and familiar, as from the cohort in Jerusalem, anxious to report, "The Chief Priest, Caiaphas sir, he told me to tell you." He catches his breath. Pontius signals a drink for the thirsty messenger.

The Prefect knowingly, "Ah ha. Caiaphas" and shakes his head, discontented, at Lefus, as much to say here comes trouble again. Lefus ever ready to attempt one upmanship, while the thirsty soldier gulps his drink provided by Shira; Lefus, to impress Shira, quick to express what he knows.

"The Passover holiday brings hundreds of thousands of pilgrims to Jerusalem." This fails to attract Shira's attention as she retreats from the Roman hierarchy.

Impatiently "Yes I know" Pontius puts down the impetuousness of Lefus.

The messenger proceeds, "Sir, the Chief Priest told me to tell you the provinces and roads to Jerusalem are blocked with the people."

Claudia's intuitions come swiftly into play, "Let Antonius keeps the peace". Lefus smiles with sarcasm.

Lefus speaks for the messenger, "The Chief Priest says your presence to protect the city is required."

Pontius ignores Lefus. "We must abandon our party for theirs!" The seated Roman couples whisper among themselves; the wives leave. He looks to Claudia with regret. Impatiently he motions to the thirsty cavalryman, with a salute and a dismissive gesture.

To Lefus Pontius says, "Send a messenger to Lucius Vitellius, the Legate of Syria; to dispatch X Legion Frentencis to Jerusalem."

Claudia faces off Pontius. "You will not go alone."

Pontius directs the Centurions, "Bring in Barabbas. Do not come back without him this time."

9
PROCESSIONS

JERUSALEM

Yeshua approaches Jerusalem, from the direct north, willingly for the Passion Week, as the Prince of Peace, adored by the crowds. Yeshua rides slowly, modestly, on an ass's young colt over palm fronds. Hundreds of exuberant pilgrims line his path. They throw palm branches to create a 'carpet,' a cushion of honor. The date, Saturday, April 24th, 28 CE, [The Chronological Gospels, Michael John Rood, Page 194] although it will become known hundreds of years into the future as "Palm Sunday." His triumphant entry into the city is an acknowledgement of His teachings and His miracles, He is the fulfilment of prophesy. Word has therefore spread throughout Judea that this man is no ordinary man.

A voice cries out in adoration. "Hosanna, blessed is the King of Israel that comes in the name of Elohim." [John 12:13]

While Pontius the Prefect of Judea, enters the city, from the north-west, reluctantly: Feared by the masses, abhorrent to most of them: Proud, in contrast, Pontius rides a fine horse. However, the real convergence of the Prefect and the perfect one will occur later. One Prefect from Rome, one perfect man from Nazareth.

As Yeshua slowly reaches the city's north wall, soft man-made clothe replace the palms. Hundreds of pilgrims lay blankets and garments before him as he enters the fish gate.

Modest on a mule, yet majestic, not everyone is pleased to see Him.

A man of greater wealth than most in this crowd will stand out with pride. Denoted by his attire, the couture of an Elder from the temple, a Pharisee, he steps forward conspicuously with arrogance and loathes this spectacle of adoration. More Pharisees arrive.

"Rabbi rebuke your disciples!" he shouts. [Luke 19:39]

Yeshua, jubilant, takes a moment to answer him. "I tell you this, if these people should hold their peace, the stones would immediately cry out." [Luke 19:40] The multitudes of pilgrims rejoice; they take solace from the correction that very few of them would dare to deliver to a member of the elite. But another lone pilgrim becomes emboldened and turns to the Pharisee to explain.

"He frees us from your rules, your traditions." Indignant, the Pharisee marches away, because he and his peers are outnumbered and unprotected. This gate into the city is at least two miles from the temple where he can cower behind Herod's soldiers and guards.

Another spectator near-by, finds the courage to shout after him, "You and your kind have added to The Torah!"

Pontius, with his armed men, comes reluctantly from Herod's Palace in Caesarea Marittima on the shores of the blue Mediterranean Sea to the dusty city. He has travelled sixty miles in a day. His duty is to make sure civil order is maintained. Backed-up with his hundreds, two cohorts, and a requisition of a thousand more soldiers from the Legate of

Syria, needed to keep the peace. Pontius needs these men for the temporary population explosion. As the pilgrims are absorbed within the walls of the city, Pontius rides his horse over the palms left strewn to cover the roadway. He cannot know the significance. The hooves of his horse may enjoy the softened road as his men trot behind. A momentary relief as they near their objective, the Antonia Fortress just two miles inside the city wall next to the temple. This will provide a rest before the tumult begins.

Interestingly, both men, Pontius and Yeshua, are on a mission. Ultimately, both men represent the desire for peace. The difference is one man enforces peace with fear and aggression yet the other, peace by order of love. They arrive with the same objective. They come together. Both bear the same basic attributes of power: The difference between the two; one of man-made power and the other divine authority. Man-made power represented with military force. The other being the complete opposite: Alone, defenseless, merciful, glorious and gracious.

When Pontius Pilate proceeds, he arrives in Jerusalem to contain the crowds; he will not know he will be an instrument of The Almighty, their YeHoVaH of Israel. The common link for the Prefect and the Prince, justice and order. Except Yeshua will inevitably provide the end result. Salvation for all who will hear Him. Pontius does not know the circumstances yet that will bring him into contrast with Yeshua.

(Footnote. Passover has a deep religious and nationalistic significance for the people. The pilgrimage brings hundreds of thousands to Jerusalem. Many of the ordinary people have come to know of Yeshua and the accurate teaching of the Torah. His open contest with the Sanhedrin, the Pharisees and the Sadducees, have made his presence contemptible to them.)

THE ANTONIA FORTRESS

In their absence from Caesarea, in range of Jerusalem, Centurions Lefus and Antonius have at long last accomplished a task set them by Pontius. They have arrested and hold Barabbas for the murders of the Hebrew elite. At this important juncture, this ritual time, it helps relieve some danger, and therefore becomes a celebration of itself. Pontius toasts his centurions and sets the next day as a time to judge Barabbas.

In the judgement hall of the Antonia Fortress, the tall, darkly handsome Barabbas, hands tied behind his back, walks in a determined manner, ahead of his two guards, flanked by Centurion Lefus. Barabbas stops defiantly in front of a seated Pontius. His high cheek bones, a structure of strength, his mature age of thirty-five gives him authority and wisdom plus a defiant contempt for the occupiers of his land. Pontius looks up at him, wide-eyed, gazes at his prisoner, to absorb his being. Pontius senses his arrogance. Lefus impatiently fills in the dead time with the obvious.

"Barabbas."

Time belongs to Pontius in such circumstances. He knows his own silence can unnerve the man to be questioned. Unlike Lefus whose impetuousness will lead to mistakes, Pontius savors his position of rule. He looks to the prisoner, now in his custody, nods his head up and down to convey this matter has a decision factor. Pontius leans back in his chair to take his time to widen his field of vision.

The slowness and quietness of his delivery exposes the strength of his position. "Ah. Ha. I've got you. The leader of the Sicarii."

The cage this man will reside in now only feet away. In moments of time, he will dwell there to contemplate his fate. Pontius takes his time so Barabbas may anticipate his own downfall. In this manner of interrogation Pontius will find the motive and justifications for these seemingly random murders. But they are not random; they are wanton violations to shake the rule of Rome. From his vibrating vocal cords, an attempt to chill the Prefect.

"This land is not your land it is ours given to us by YeHoVaH."

"That debate was settled by Rome."

The Prefect of Judea knows their independence came to an end ninety years ago when Damascus and Jerusalem were conquered by the Romans in 63 B.C.E. He sits back in his chair to tempt forth anxious statements out of his prisoner that will either be defensive or incriminatory.

A spittle filled burst of reverberating air from Barabbas sprays the vicinity, "Yehudim who collaborate with Rome: Treason. Death!"

He goads him casually with, "One who murders his own says this?" Pontius stands and walks around Barabbas as a predator may circle his weak victim, intends to strike and kill, waits for the best moment.

"The punishment for treason is death" sounds like an admission of guilt to Pontius. Although Barabbas operates zealously as a patriot and without doubt holds himself above reproach by this mere gentile. Nonchalantly, "Then you have convicted yourself" and Pontius sits down again.

The prisoner protests, "YeHoVaH is my judge" is the perfect entry for Pontius to summon up his humor.

"Then today, in his absence, I will sentence you" which angers Barabbas.

"One day our mighty and victorious king will come" which amuses the judge, the ridiculousness causes him to snigger and huff at Barabbas.

"Our Messiah will squash you and your Roman Empire, like the cockroaches you are."

"Oh. And how will he do that?"

"At his coming and by His Glorious might." Pontius can only laugh at him, but Barabbas wants the last word. "Our Messiah will come as a warrior!" Barabbas says. Defiant, he turns and walks away.

Pontius stands, wide-eyed. The two guards grab his arms, Barabbas resists, and they struggle. Centurion Lefus holds a dagger to the prisoner's belly. The guards force him around to face Pontius.

"Your sentence is death by crucifixion. Take him away."

The guards struggle to drag him out. Centurion Lefus smiles a triumph over Barabbas as he leaves. Pontius will stay the execution until it suits him politically. In the meantime, the soldiers may have this dagger man for some time. He will be interrogated again, this time by Lefus, to make him give up the identities and locations of the other younger men in The Sicarii. The Elite will see that Barabbas the assassin, in Roman custody, will be served up as a political prize. Pontius hopes Caiaphas will acknowledge that Rome has done its job to protect the people and maintain peace.

10
TEMPLE

JERUSALEM

After judgement upon Barabbas in Jerusalem, Pontius resettles comfortably into the palace built by Herod the Great, provided by Antipas. Not that Antipas had much choice in the matter. The Prefect requisitioned these premises customarily, "seize and occupy!" Antipas, being a friend of Rome, cooperated without hesitation.

Approximately one-third of a mile separates the Antonia Fortress from this palace which is about in the middle of the Upper City. Some six-tenths of a mile from the Antonia Fortress to Antipas's other, larger palace. The large palace on the western side of the city sits high on the "South Western Hill." The temple is estimated to be one-quarter of a mile from the small palace where Pontius resides in the Upper City. Walking distances between these buildings varies from seven minutes to about fifteen minutes. Present for Passover, the huge extra crowds of pilgrims who squeeze into the city will hinder and slow down this journey time to make it longer.

Yeshua walks stridently through the busy streets to pass beautiful dancers and passionate musicians near the temple. They too want to capitalize, hold out for rewards. He pays no regard to the bare midriffs of the dancers that jiggle to attract the crowd. Near the temple, the booths, stalls and tables line the thoroughfare. The hustle and bustle of a market, the tinkle of the money replaces the dancers' castanets and livestock makes a cacophony of noises; bleating lambs, cages of doves cuckoo, and goats stamp their hooves, tethered, make false charges; sometimes a horn catches a garment and rips it, to the annoyance of the wearer.

Pilgrims, some in ragged garments, others in better attire, give up their Roman coins, foreign coins or coins showing images of faces, etc., in exchange for the temple coins. The wealthy money-exchangers cannot fail to make more money; it is voluminous. Yeshua stops at a table to observe the commerce. He monitors the faces of those well-dressed men who exchange coins. He reads them as avaricious, gleeful, they bag success, which is easy for them in this monopoly, this corporate control. (While those who give up the contents of their purses look downcast, downtrodden, and crestfallen at the excessive expense of it all.)

In turn the tradesmen accept those temple coins for the purchase of sacrificial doves and lambs. More profit for them increases poverty for the pilgrims. A lamb, a sacrificial offer, will later become their expensive dinner. The city and countryside will be smoky with cooked meat on open fires. Yeshua carefully monitors the transactions as the tradesmen sense His presence. They look up uneasily at this mysterious observer who follows every detail. Yeshua gazes continuously toward the acquisitive. Those who take money from the pilgrims become more uneased by His concentration.

His presence in front of the money-exchangers and tradesmen causes them to glance up and become more and more uneasy. Business continues. Yeshua walks up and down the lanes of commerce within the temple grounds. A large area and the bustle of business is a constant with lots of buying and selling activity. The act of passing money and sacrificial goods becomes halting as the tradesmen's glances are taken in by the figure of a man whose authority comes down from above. One-man glances skyward as a lone cloud passes a shadow over his table. (Not the cloud but the man who stands before him casts that shadow!) In the doorways of the temple, Pharisees and Sadducees watch the man they think they may know by reputation. Whatever the case, they are drawn to the uneasy atmosphere he brings.

Suddenly, all fury and flailing take place in a whirlwind of angry upheaval. Yeshua moves in to turn the tables upside down, spills their wares, coins scatter, doves take flight; lambs break loose and run amok; the peddlers, astonished, look spell-bound, frozen in disbelief.

Figures lurk in the background, drip in gold-braided clothes, they wear the scales of serpents. The rich "vipers" Pharisees and Sadducees; silent tongues, venomous teeth, look on with loathsome indignation. Their under-the-breath disapproval made deadly silent by Yeshua when he shouts so all may hear,

"Is it not written, my House shall be called The House of Prayer for all 'peoples.'" [Matt. 21:13 & Mark 11:17]

He overturns another table and chases the traders away, snatches their purses and throws them down to the ground as they run.

Yeshua screams, "But you have made it a den of thieves!!!" [Matt. 21:13 & Mark 11:17] The visiting pilgrims are at first stunned then see the coins strewn on the ground and dive down to grab the most they can. Their gathering inhibits the tradesmen who attempt reclamation. Yeshua's statement frightens the traders, many of whom hastily gather whatever they can, and leave in haste. Former customers, leave, while a few others draw near to Yeshua in silent wonderment. The Pharisees and Sadducees slither and disappear within the temple. They have seen and heard all that they need to. These are the same faces previously seen plotting with Caiaphas against Yeshua.

While some slink and shuffle away, Yeshua stands in the midst unharmed, not reproached but seen by all and made speechless. His defiant stance is still, and His serenity cannot be contested. Out of the shadows more Pharisees and Sadducees emerge, more familiar faces.

CAIAPHAS'S PALACE

They re-appear before Caiaphas and meet together with Annas at the palace belonging to the High Priest. They report the tumult they witnessed in their temple. A sacrilege: A disruption of their business. (They sanction in accord with *their* man-made rules, which *they* bend to suit their own ends, the business practices that keep them rich, but they never admit it.) Most of those present are against this imposter who proclaims himself a Rabbi and more. One Pharisee expressly confirms the man alters the minds of the common people. Their insinuations against this troublemaker include witchcraft, demon worship, and blatant infractions displayed with the bold disrespect of their laws. But two men of this Elite corps are there to defend him.

Joseph of Arimathea contends that Yeshua is a man of peace and non-violence. Caiaphas reminds him there were many witnesses to his violent temper, smashed tables, thrown purses, kicked traders and money-exchangers, shoving people down on their knees to make them grovel before him. He distorts the truth, he lies.

The Sadducee concedes some of the unrest, but he also knows their testimony against the Rabbi began as an exaggeration and they have taken the argument beyond reason. He may claim to be divine or a prophet but the main cause for their concern is that he gains a following that will become hostile against the Sanhedrin and The Council. "The common people take up his cause, and they, in their turn, become his weapon against us."

Nicodemus, a friend of Joseph, both of whom have had an encounter with Yeshua adds, "He speaks only of peace and love, and he removes the old lies, to bring us truth."

Caiaphas and his clique look upon the likes of Nicodemus and Joseph as if they have been completely taken in and fallen under the spell of the trickster and therefore should be treated accordingly. They look with disdain upon the two who advocate being born of the spirit, a concept beyond their belief: Joseph defends his position, "Those who are lost thirst in the desert. Those who are found are quenched by the everlasting water."

The Chief Priest contends with those philosophical thoughts: These two men are a perfect example of brainwashing, he thinks. This small sample shows the dangerous man Yeshua proffers his teachings. The ignorant, swayed, their lackadaisical minds will be an on-going danger unless addressed quickly, now. Caiaphas, indignant that this insubordination should be dealt with on all levels, makes his decree.

"Caesar Tiberius wants peace with our people. Our position is also peace. Therefore. we must use our influence on the Prefect," Caiaphas says. The plot evolves to eliminate the threat Yeshua poses. The planned elimination of Yeshua takes another step into the darkness now as Caiaphas brings his conforming Elite members to follow his directions.

11
VISION

THE PALACE

The top of the wall at Herod's palace on high ground gives a panoramic view of the city below. Throngs of pilgrims course through the streets as the red sun slides down over the horizon behind Pontius. He looks east but he cannot see inside the walls of the temple where the merchants and money men re-erect their stalls to prepare for more business. Servicing the late arrivals will be their last opportunity for profit before Passover. Pontius enters the building to enjoy a quiet evening with Claudia.

Earlier Claudia spoke with Antonius about his young servant boy who was healed. This has caught the imagination of the wife of the Prefect so much so that she walked to the fortress with Shira, and an escort, to see for herself. No explanation can be given. Antonius specifically asked that this miracle worker stay away but give his word. The servant was completely healed in an instant. The account would befuddle Centurion Lefus if told. Antonius had done what he was told to do by the Prefect, "Keep it quiet lest you become a mockery" was the advice he took. Claudia makes good dinner conversation out of this phenomenal account. Pontius, ever the practical man, puts it down to simple coincidence.

They retire. Claudia Procula sleeps: She tosses and turns next to Pontius. He lies awake, watches her. Claudia, lying on her back, her hand reaches toward Pontius but makes no contact, retracts. He continues to observe strange unconscious movements.

THE GARDEN OF GETHSEMANE

A hand reaches under his civilian garments to grip the handle of his sword. The cause of this man's alerted state comes clearly into view. About five miles away to the east, the other side of the temple, there in the garden of Gethsemane, quiet, dark and still, this vision enters Claudia's sleep. Simon Peter, a follower of Yeshua, prepares to defend his Master.

During the night, Wednesday, April 28th 28 CE [The Chronological Gospels. CKJV Michael John Rood, Page 229 & 234]: Brandishing swords and staves, the Temple Guards in fine livery, the Scribes, the Elders and Priests, approach with torches and lanterns. A young man, naked but with a linen cloth draped about him lingers and moves in the peripheral background. Yeshua, face unseen, stands his ground, while the force appears to stop, impotent. One man, Yehudas, walks forward, hesitatingly. The disciples stand with and behind Yeshua. They look on, concerned. Yehudas says, "Hail Master," and kisses Yeshua on the cheek. [Matt. 26:49]

Yeshua waits a moment and while no explanation comes forth, he asks what he already knows. "Friend, what is the reason you have come?" [Matt. 26:50] Yehudas turns away, leaves, unable to face up to his mission. Yeshua knows everything so he presses another question to the official arresting party.

"You come out with swords and staves as against a thief?" [Matt.26:55]

The young man approaches Yeshua, lays hold on him, not aggressively but possessively. His presence, a curiosity that defies an answer: "When I was daily with you in the Temple, teaching, you stretched forth no hands against me." [Matt. 26:55. Luke 22:53. Mark 14:49] The Temple Guard, for all their might, remains tongue-tied. "But this is your hour, and the power of darkness." [Luke 22:53] He waits again but they make no move against him. "The scriptures must be fulfilled." [Matt. 26:54. Mark 14:49] The young man releases his hold and runs. As the young man flees his linen cloth falls away; he runs naked.

(The young man symbolizes our coming to Yeshua and leaving ourselves exposed to his knowledge of us and all that we do. Yeshua sees through us as if naked and transparent hiding nothing and many of us run from Him. Many who flee from Him do so in fear of losing the will for their own lives.)

THE PALACE

In the bedchamber at Herod's palace Claudia suddenly awakes. Pontius rolls over groaning. Claudia sits up eyes wide open she sees something. Excessively bound in ropes, blurry, Yeshua stands motionless, face obscured. Pontius turns over again. A breeze passes by. A vacuous space: Claudia stares into the empty infinity of darkness. Whispers in awe, "The Rabbi," Quietly, "The Rabbi." Pontius stirs to consciousness. "The Rabbi has been arrested."
Pontius rubs his eyes, looks at her.

"How do you know? You dream about the one who performs tricks?" Claudia ignores him.

She sees darkly, Pontius, Claudia and Antonius approach Joseph of Arimathea who holds the burial shroud.

Pontius rolls over, sees nothing, and buries his head. "You've had a bad dream."

Claudia remains transfixed.

The Trial of Yeshua
ACTUAL LOCATIONS, JERUSALEM

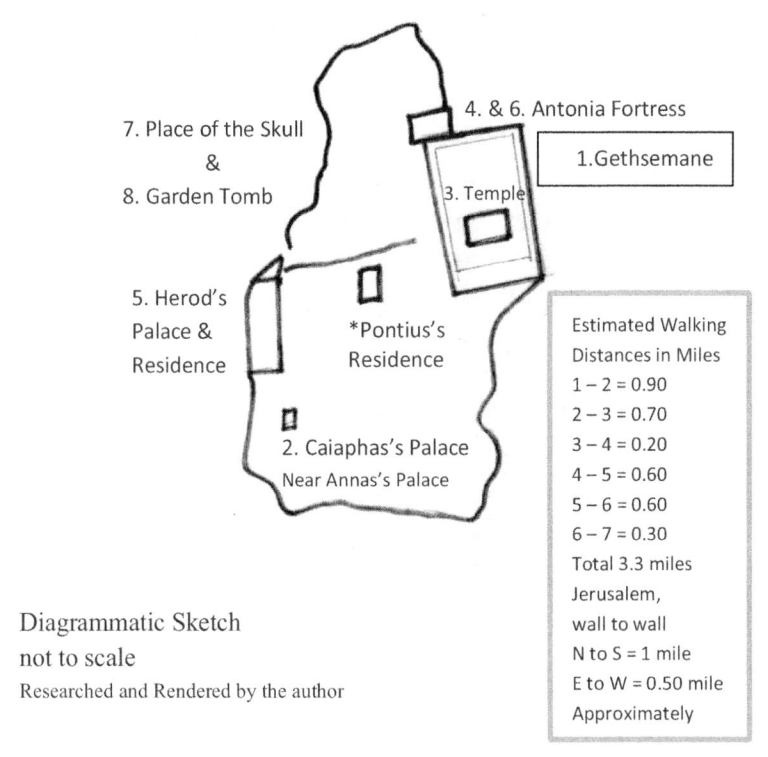

7. Place of the Skull
&
8. Garden Tomb

4. & 6. Antonia Fortress

1. Gethsemane

3. Temple

5. Herod's Palace & Residence

*Pontius's Residence

2. Caiaphas's Palace
Near Annas's Palace

Estimated Walking Distances in Miles
1 – 2 = 0.90
2 – 3 = 0.70
3 – 4 = 0.20
4 – 5 = 0.60
5 – 6 = 0.60
6 – 7 = 0.30
Total 3.3 miles
Jerusalem, wall to wall
N to S = 1 mile
E to W = 0.50 mile
Approximately

Diagrammatic Sketch
not to scale
Researched and Rendered by the author

Numerical sequence shows the physical progression of the arrest, trial, execution and death of Yeshua Ha Mashiach which transpired during the night and morning of Wednesday, April 28th 28 CE. From beginning to end, a duration of twelve hours. [The Chronological Gospels, pages 229 – 258] *Pontius's Residence at Herod Antipas's 'other' palace. The Palace of Annas was on the Southwestern Hill near Caiaphas's Palace.

12
TRIAL

THE PALACE

The night before, Pontius alone looks out from the top of the wall, Herod's Palace. The throngs of pilgrims make their way into the city. The sun slowly descends toward the horizon. Before leaving Rome to take up this rule he had a mandate, to respect the traditions of the Yehudim. (The Passover celebration he knows a little about.) The last two Passovers were without incident. This time he senses viscerally, uneasiness in the air.

The origin of this festival goes back to the time the Israelites escaped from Egyptian slavery. The Almighty YeHoVaH warned His Israelites that he would take the life of every first born Egyptian. To protect His own people from the Angel of Death, they were instructed to sacrifice a lamb and place the blood on the lintel of their homes as a sign that their children would be saved by the Passover.

The next time Pontius sees the sun come up it will be the beginning of a new day and a new age in history. The Prefect will be in an impossible situation. A position that proves there are forces greater than any individual, regardless of their stature in life, regardless of what they believe. The will of good providence prevails even though the life of a pagan Roman may be the least likely candidate. YeHoVaH knows best. The red sun slides down over the horizon, signals the end of another day. Intangible, unseen forces between the good of light and the evil of darkness will commence battle soon.

THE GARDEN OF GETHSEMANE (1)

Yeshua knows everything so he presses the question. "You come out with swords and staves as against a thief?" [Matt. 26:55]

Yeshua steps forward and they step back in fear, stumble and fall to the ground. This passive man controls the situation. His aura so powerful, the force of it renders them helpless.

"Whom do you seek?" [John 18:4 & 7]

A few voices mumble together as they regain their footing. "Yeshua of Nazareth" [John 18:5]

"I am he." [John 18:5] The arresting parties, still in a state of paralysis, appear reluctant, amazingly unsure of what they are to do. "I have told you that I am he. Therefore, if you seek me, let these go away." [John 18:8] He gestures for his disciples to leave.

One disciple rushes forward, Peter, his sword revealed, suddenly, sword-cut-swipes the right ear off a Jewish servant, Malcus. The ear hangs, bloodily, by some remaining flesh on his neck. Yeshua moves forward quickly, touches the ear and miraculously replaces it. "Permit even this." [Luke 22:51] Simultaneously, the blood disappears. The crowd, unmoved, still impotent, stunned, still do nothing! Even those who plainly see the miracle are blinded to it. Yeshua turns to the aggressor, Peter. "Put your sword into the sheath. All who take the sword will perish by the sword." [John 18:11. Matt. 26:52]

"The cup my Father has given me, shall I not drink from it?" [John 18:11]

Even those who plainly see the miracle are blinded to it. Yeshua turns to the aggressor, Simon Peter. He looks with compassion at Peter while Peter remains transfixed.

Yeshua turns to face The Council and the Temple Officer face on. With pointed authority he exclaims, "All who take up the sword will perish by the sword. If I prayed to my Father, he would immediately send twelve legions of angels." [Matt. 26:52 & 53] Yet still they hesitate. Yeshua asks them again, "So that the scriptures of the prophets will be fulfilled, the cup that my Father has given me, shall I not drink from it?" [John 18:11]

Then the Temple Officers become impulsive with vigor, they respond to the insult that this man, this lowly carpenter, claims his place in prophecy. They overly bind a submissive Yeshua: Being jostled roughly as if trying to tie-up a wild animal Yeshua remains calm and quiet. The disciples, in fear for them, given their freedom by Yeshua, flee in haste, run from the garden. The arresting parties pull and tug at Yeshua. He is forced to pick up their pace.

ANNAS'S PALACE

Yeshua and the group arrive outside Annas's large house. Pushed disrespectfully by the Temple Officers toward the doorway while Annas appears with another person to block their entry, Yeshua receives no civility from the former chief priest. Intent conversation, at close quarters, takes place in hushed and muffled tones. Evidently, Annas knows all there is to know about this man as the conspiracy ominously unfolds. They do not want to alert the neighbors. Annas motions them to leave.

HEROD'S PALACE

Claudia, restless, still in a semi-trance, wanders Herod's palace. She enters one of the anterooms with stealth.

CAIAPHAS'S PALACE (2)

Inside the grand palace owned by Caiaphas, a core of representatives stands to face Yeshua. Caiaphas and his council convene to further the plot. Noticeably absent are the two men who previously defended the Rabbi and pointed out the malfeasance in the manipulation of their laws and codes of justice in this covert manner: Nicodemus and Joseph of Arimathea would surely object if they had been included. Caiaphas looks around at the false witnesses but none of them steps forward, so he fixates on one to speak, urges him with intense stares and anxiously nods for him to begin.

"We heard him say, 'I am able to destroy the Temple of YeHoVaH made with hands and build another in three days without hands.'" [Matthew 26:61 & Mark 14:58] All eyes turn angrily upon Yeshua. The hour has passed the middle of the night on Wednesday, April 28th, 28 CE.

Caiaphas takes up the prosecutorial role, "Have you no answer to make? What is it that these men testify against you?" [Matthew 26:62 & Mark 14:60] Yeshua remains silent and motionless. "I adjure you by the living Elohim that you tell us whether you be the Messiah, the Son of Elohim?" [Matthew 26:63]

Yeshua, seen from behind, pans the group. His eyes lock on every person present.

Calmly Yeshua states confirmation; "You have rightly spoken. Nevertheless, I say to you, hereafter shall you see the Son of Man sitting on the right hand of the Almighty, coming in the clouds of heaven." [Matthew 26:64 & Mark 14:62]

Caiaphas rips his own garment with righteous indignation! "He has spoken blasphemy! What further need have we of witnesses? Behold you have heard his blasphemy!
What do you think?" [Matthew 26:65 & Mark 14:63] All those present speak as one voice, as if rehearsed.

"He is guilty and deserving death." [Matthew 26:66 & Mark 14:64]

HEROD'S PALACE

In Herod's Palace bed chamber Claudia looks upon Pontius while he sleeps.

CAIAPHAS'S PALACE

Yeshua now stands bound with a previously added blindfold while Caiaphas continues to interrogate him. "What about your disciples and your teachings?" [John 18:19]

"I spoke openly to the world. I always taught in the synagogues and in the Temple where these Pharisees assemble. I have said nothing in secret. Why do you ask me? Ask these who heard me what I said to them - look they know what I said." [John 18:20 & 21]

One of the council steps forward and slaps Yeshua across the face with the palm of his hand. Yeshua recoils. "You answer the Chief Priest like that!?" [John 18:22]

"If I have spoken evil, bear witness to the evil. But if I have spoken truth, why do you strike me?" [John 18:23]

"Prophesy to us!" Another strike on Yeshua who turns the other cheek to await more abuse.

"You Messiah. Prophesy. Who is it that struck you?" [Luke 22.64 & Matthew 26.67] They wait. Yeshua does not answer. Others degradingly slap him with an open hand. Some cowardly beat him with their fists. They disgustingly spit in his face. [Mark 14:65 Matthew 26:67 & 68 & Luke 22:64] Yeshua remains silent, blindfolded, motionless.

THE TEMPLE (3)

The Temple Hall made from hewn stone gradually lightens as the dawn breaks. Blindfolded, Yeshua stands motionless: The council chamber swells with scores of the ruling Sanhedrin and Yeshua's accusers. An outburst ... [Matthew 15:1] "Are you the Messiah?" [Luke 22:67]

"Even if I tell you, you still will not believe, and if I were to ask you, you would neither answer me nor let me go. But this I will say when this is over, the Son of Man shall sit on the right hand of the Almighty." [Luke 22:67.68.69]

The group together asks him, "Are you then the Son of Elohim?" [Luke 22:70]

"You said it." [Luke 22:70]

Pleased to accept the confession, the Council Members band together, "What need do we have to any further witnesses? We ourselves have heard it from his own mouth." [Luke 22:71]

Roman soldiers appear. The High Priests, Scribes, Council Members and a total group of some fifty-plus, includes Temple Guards, speak blubberingly and abusively as they push the bound figure of the man Yeshua. The early morning light of dawn invades the ominous shadows of the approaching group. They keep pushing and pulling the blindfolded Yeshua toward the Antonia Fortress.

THE ANTONIA FORTRESS (4)

"Blasphemer, death for the Nazarene, the penalty for blasphemy is death. He has brought it upon himself." Without resistance, Yeshua is shoved into the building, as the angry group stops short of the entrance. The Temple Guards hand signal two Roman Soldiers to push Yeshua further inside. The Romans acknowledge the Temple Guards have a prisoner and take custody of the passive man. One of the Roman soldiers dispatches a mounted messenger and the Prefect's horse to Pontius at the palace.

HEROD'S PALACE

Claudia walks from the anti-room, to the bed chamber to shake Pontius out of his sleep.

He hears voices, looks astonished and gets out of bed. Claudia tells her husband a messenger has come from the fortress in haste with news that a large delegation, and a prisoner, demands his presence. Ruffled, Pontius fastens his uniform about his stocky figure.

THE ANTONIA FORTRESS (4)

By-passing the assembly at the entrance to the fortress, Pontius's horses' hooves cut the air with a sudden silence. He enters the Judgement Hall of the Antonia Fortress with a flurry. The bound, blindfolded Yeshua stands between two Roman soldiers.

Pontius barks, "What is it, that it cannot wait until daybreak?" He gestures impatiently for the blindfold to be removed from the prisoner and dismounts. Mus, on a pony, having caught up, grab the reins of the Prefect's horse and leads it away.

Immediately one of the Roman soldiers, Acilius, removes the rags that blindfold the Rabbi. He says, "The Yehudim outside have complaints against this man." Pontius looks closely at Yeshua, and then struts back and forth.

"Who is he?"

Ignoring the question he cannot answer, "They are waiting to see you sire," Acilius adds quickly. Pontius looks at Yeshua, again: Stares.

"Well. Get them in here," he says with impatience.

Acilius explains, "They are about to celebrate their Passover."

"Let them in!"

Acilius hesitates to elaborate, "They cannot come in. They believe they will defile themselves."

Pontius moves his stare away from Yeshua, building some anger, "Huh. I know. I know. They make up their own laws! So, is this Yehudi not contaminated? Now that he is already in our company!" He looks back at the silent, motionless Yeshua. "Who is this man?"

Acilius says, "Yeshua, the son of a carpenter." Pontius huff and puffs and *struts out of the Judgement Hall,* out of the building to the courtyard entrance where he stops in front of the growing and restless group. Caiaphas lingers in the background.

An anonymous voice within the group blurts out, "The blasphemer must be dealt with today."

Pontius glares at them. "What accusations do you bring against this man?" [Luke 23:29]

Two women, Mary Magdalen and Mary, mother of James, move cautiously through the restless group. They know their presence is not just unwanted but plainly ignored.

"If this man were *not* an evil-doer, we would *not* have handed him over to you." [Luke 23:30 & John 18:30]

Growing frustration: Pontius looks around for the voice. Pontius mumbles his thoughts, "'Evil-doer' is not an offense I can charge him with." He looks at the group who seem impotent. He raises his authoritative tone and asks, "Who speaks against this man?"

He spots the very familiar face near to him and looks stone-like at Caiaphas. Now angled on the Chief Priest he zeros his fierier words clearly at the real offender before him. "Take him yourselves and judge him according to your own laws." [Luke 23:31 & John 18:36] Caiaphas knows a challenge when he hears it. Pontius turns his back on them, walks.

Caiaphas looks defiant and nudges a Council Member who stands next to him to say, "It is not lawful for us to put a man to death." [Luke 23:31 & John 18:31]

His departure comes to a full stop. Pontius turns, looks at them, and measures them. "Nothing you have said would lead me to believe he has committed a serious crime."

Caiaphas looks knowingly at the scribe nearest to him on the other side who is encouraged to speak up.

"We found this man inciting the people to rebellion against Caesar." [Luke 23:2]

The Council Member qualifies the charge, "He does not pay tribute to Caesar." [Luke 23:2]

The two women with earnest expectancy look toward Pontius and see in him a desire to be a fair judge. He shakes his head, "What is it exactly that you accuse him of?" [John 18:29] Caiaphas plants the seeds of a poison that is being concocted against an innocent man; at long last he states the complaint in a half-truth.

"He claims he is The Messiah, The King, instead of Caesar." [Luke 23:2]

For one brief moment the two women catch the eye of Pontius the only antidote to the poisoned seeds of discontent around them. They are in fear of saying anything because the council rules with the complexities of oral law they would use to blast away at anyone's objections. Nevertheless, these two women know exactly who Yeshua is! Pontius amused, mutters, "Ah Huh! Lunacy," Pontius, shakes his head in total disbelief, turns away, *and reenters the Judgement Hall* to look again upon this mystery man.

Flushed, Pontius walks up to the face of Yeshua. He has spoken publicly outside, now he assumes his private persona in an attempt to strike at a personal cord. "Are you the King of The Yehudim?" [Mark 1:2 Luke 23:3 & John 18:33]

Acilius, the Roman soldier, joined by the Roman soldiers, Tarraco, Creticus, and Cicero, a clique who disrespect their Prefect. They see him as a man who could have killed off this trouble-maker Caiaphas in this very courtyard when the priest objected to the shields honoring Tiberius Caesar. Now the Chief Priest has come back to challenge Pontius again. These three Roman thugs press their lips together to prevent a smirk. Good fortune for them at this point in time means Pontius is too busy to note their insubordination. Acilius sees it and refrains from joining in. Their future punishment will not be without pain, suffering and death.

Yeshua answers quietly with confidence, "Do you say this of your own accord, or do others say it to you, about me?" [John 18:34] Pontius takes a step back in surprised astonishment.

"Am I a Yehudi?" [John 18:35] Am I a Jew?" Pontius calms himself, goes into thought mode. Should he be concerned for the foolishness of this group? "Your own people, the Chief Priest, they have handed you over to me; what have you done?" [John 18:35]

"My kingdom is not of this world; if it were of this world, my servants would fight that I might not be handed over to the chief priests, scribes, Council Members, and Pharisees." [John 18:36] Pontius quietly listens as Yeshua continues with a consolidation of who he is. "Do you think that I cannot appeal to my Father, and he will at once send twelve legions of angels?" [Matthew 26:53] Pontius raises his eyebrows incredulously. "But my kingdom is not of this world." [John 18:36] Pontius moves forward, looks for Yeshua's sanity.

"Ah. Ha. So, you are a king?" [John 18:37] Pontius notices early dawn gives way to sunrise; rays of light enter the anteroom and illuminate Yeshua in silhouette. Pontius strains to see his face.

"For this I was born, and for this I have come into the world, to bear witness to the **truth**." With accusatory emphasis Yeshua adds, "You say that I am a king. Everyone who is of the **truth** hears my voice." [John 18:37]

Pontius circles Yeshua thoughtfully and looks at the direction from which rays of blinding light enter: Then shields his eyes to ask privately. "What is **truth**?" [John 18:38] Yeshua turns his head as Pontius circles. Pontius stops, waits for an answer. He looks into Yeshua's eyes, shakes his head and waits longer for an answer to his question. He then struts out.

(The question was answered by Yeshua in brief. But Pontius wanted to learn more. However, Yeshua's long answer to the question would by necessity have to take on a heavenly explanation.

This day has a time limit. Yeshua's divine timing will keep on track to fulfill the complex matters of prophecy and destiny.)

At the entrance to the stone courtyard the sun illuminates the 'quiet' group. Pontius marches up to face them close-up and deliver his verdict.

"I find no fault in this man." [Luke 23:4 & John 18:38]

The group makes noises, mutterings. Pontius looks around the group. They counter, "He blasphemes against our YeHoVaH."

One of the outspoken Council Members adds, "He instigates trouble among the people teaching throughout the land from Galilee to Jerusalem!" [Luke 23:5]

Pontius looks at the group for reason. "Is this man a Galilean?"

"Yes."

The Prefect immediately sees an escape from this difficult situation. "Then he comes under Herod Antipas' jurisdiction." Pontius swiftly turns back into the building. Enters the judgement hall hurriedly blusteringly, he stops short of Yeshua and ponders the man before him for a quiet moment, looks for a way to prevent judgement by King Herod Antipas, a man of many character flaws. "Have you no answers?" Yeshua remains silent. [Mark 15:5] Pontius marvels.
[Matthew 27:14]

Removing his dagger he says, "Do you hear how many

things they testify against you?" [Matthew 27:13 & Mark 15:4]

With astonishment [Mark 15:5] at this man's reserve and stately demeanor he slaps the blade of the dagger in his open hand. "Why are you saying nothing?" [Mark 15:4] He turns to the soldiers and gestures with his dagger, "remove his bindings!"

In a private appeal, he speaks very quietly, "Are you going to incite a rebellion? But against whom? Tiberius Caesar? The Roman Empire? The Chief Priests?" He sheathes his dagger. "You don't pay your taxes? You are a Rabbi or a king!? So, you will depose King Herod Antipas?" Pontius waits for answers. None are forthcoming. He is left; it would seem to him, to have the alternative; to send Yeshua to King Herod Antipas to pass the burden of justice to him. Attempting to do it gladly, he dispatches them, but an uncanny concern tackles the Prefect's consciousness. Pontius would like to think this will be the end of the matter, but he can only hope.

HEROD'S RESIDENCE (5)

Caiaphas, the council, the Temple Guards, the whole group, all stand outside the other larger palace, in a huddle, ready to heckle the king. Inside one of the main rooms, behind the back of Yeshua, King Herod Antipas stands listening to the mob outside. Inside, Herod's Officers of War always stand behind Herod to protect him. He cocks his head as he hears from the outside, "Blasphemer, death to the blasphemer, the penalty is death!"

Centurion Lefus stands-by Yeshua as Antipas with no need to be serious, ridicules this regal imposter. "Ha ha ha! I have heard so much about you. Now my new friend the Prefect sends you to me." Outside Antipas hears a voice shout, "He has brought it upon himself."

"Ha ha ha. The Prefect wants to show me, you are no different than any one of those out there." Antipas looks to his Officers of War for approval, who laugh [Luke 23:8, 9, 10] just to please him as they always do. Herod Antipas walks toward a draped, hanging gorgeous, radiant robe. Smiling at Lefus and then turning to Yeshua he says, "I would be convinced if he would bring just one angel for us to see." Yeshua begins to turn slowly. Antipas pleads with mockery in his voice, "Just one miracle?" [Luke 23:8] Antipas remains in a frivolous mood unable to detect the solemn deity of this man in his presence: Yeshua remains silent and reserved, not bowing one fraction of a measurement to concede. Then with great pleasure Herod arrays Yeshua in the glorious and magnificent robe. [Luke 23:11 & 12] Antipas had his fun. No doubt with the death of John on his mind, the puppet king does not want to be responsible and condemn another innocent man: He will return the favor to The Prefect so he may punish Him.

THE ANTONIA FORTRESS (6)

The incandescent white robe reflects on the Roman uniforms as Yeshua is led by Lefus back into the courtyard at the Antonia Fortress. At ground level, Pontius makes haste, readies himself, having heard the commotion approach, the chattering accusatory group has grown like ants trailing the sweetness of nectar they wish to consume. Determined, Pontius walks to Yeshua, followed by Centurions Antonius. His heavy steps would squash those ants, if he could.

Pontius gestures impatiently to the Roman soldiers, Acilius, Tarraco, Creticus and Cicero, to take hold of Yeshua and to get him inside, while Pontius remains outside to calm the crowd. He raises his hands to quiet them. The two women, Mary Magdalen and Mary, mother of James and Yeshua appear anxious. He directs his gaze at Caiaphas and raises his voice in his public manner.

"You brought me this man as one who was perverting the people; and after examining him before you, I do not find the man guilty of your charges against him." [Luke 23:14] He swings around to leave.

Murmurs within the group come. "He plans to destroy the temple."

Pontius stops and swings back around bodily annoyed at the comment, ignoring the idiocy of the claim.

He raises his voice further, "Neither did Herod Antipas!!! He sent him back to me!!!" [Luke 23:15]

Retaliatory outbursts of, "Death to the blasphemer!" further angers Pontius as these people keep challenging his better judgement, he looks at them with disgust. Yeshua and the soldiers, are no longer visible, they have gone inside. The two women, Mary Magdalen and Mary, mother of James, look to Pontius pleadingly as their only hope for Yeshua.

"Nothing deserving death has been done by him!!!" [Luke 23:15]

The two women, with optimism, look around them to see angry men. The group becomes a mob and shouts their objections.

"He threatens Rome."

Pontius spins again to exit and fumes to Lefus: "Bring out a cohort and have them readied here to disperse this mob." He continues to the Judgement Seat. [Matthew 27:19]

Followed by Antonius, mumbling concerns, "That confounded Tribune and his Legion, where are they?"

Annas, steps out in front of Pontius, "Prefect. On this day, the feast of the Passover, you can release one prisoner, anyone we request."

Centurion Lefus approaches with a small scroll.

"Yes. You will have me release to you, The King of the Yehudim?" [Mark 15:9]

Lefus puts the small scroll into Pontius's hand.

Annas quickly corrects the Prefect, "No not him, Barabbas." [John 18:40]

Stunned, Pontius fumes ash gray. Ignores Annas. Pontius unrolls the scroll. [Matthew 27:19] He reads with intense interest. While the crowd gets noisier. As he reads the message to himself, he hears the author's voice, Claudia, very clearly in his mind. "Have nothing to do with that just man! Today, I was greatly afflicted in a dream because of him." [Matthew 27:19] He recalls the night, Claudia's disturbed presence of mind, her body movements, her restless wanderings. She is greatly troubled, yet he is faced with practical decisions. He refuses to be distracted.

A fragment of fact and fairmindedness may yet remain. He addresses the mob. "Which of these two do you want me to release to you?" [Matthew 27:20] Listeners within this Mob pick-up the name Barabbas and repeat it.

"Barabbas, Barabbas, Barabbas."

"What shall I then do with Yeshua, who is called Messiah?" [Matthew 27:22 & Mark 15:12] Pontius re-rolls the scroll as the content burdens his conscience. He stands erect.

The mob is relentless, "Let him be crucified." [Matthew 27:22 & Mark 15:13] The two women, Mary Magdalen and Mary, mother of James, look to Pontius again ever pleadingly. He is their only hope to correct this travesty of justice.

"Why, what evil has he done?" [Mark 15:14] Pontius, white-faced, impatience now quietly raging within, shakes his head, picks up speed and strides to the Judgement Hall.

Yeshua stands patiently, flanked by the soldiers, and waits. Outside, the noisy crowd builds from a ripple to a waterfall. He hears them shout.

"Barabbas, Barabbas, Barabbas!"

Pontius walks up to Yeshua and with increasing vexation says, "Why do you just stand there saying nothing? Do you not hear the many things they witness against you?" [Matthew 27:13 & Mark 15:4]

Pontius marvels at his silence, and then with growing frustration he faces Yeshua more intensely. [Mark 15:5] "They demand the release of Barabbas. His penalty is death. SO that YOU should suffer HIS punishment!!! What kind of justice is this?" He waits for Yeshua to speak but he does not. [Matthew 27:14]

"Huh?" Exasperated, Pontius leaves.

Pontius walks out onto the top of the wall, looks down into the courtyard, to view the crowd. Centurion Antonius stands-by the Prefect awaiting his decision. The vista provided by the fortress shows the day comes alive with a growing number of people entering the gates of the city. The cohort of Roman troops march up to the face of the fortress at ground level and line the outside walls ominously. The mob grows silent. Pontius sits down on a seat and pulls at a desk, taking his time to carefully assess the situation. The crowd starts-up again, chants, from mumbles to shouts.

"Barabbas, Barabbas, Barabbas!" Their murmurs and mumbles begin the babble of buzzing flies. He turns toward Antonius.

"Bring Barabbas and The Rabbi up here." Pontius looks out to see more people join the mob. His mind is busy with assessments. He has a few minutes to run through a projection of possibilities that may take place down there. His men are outnumbered. Nevertheless, they are well armed.

The crowd has nothing with which to fight except religious fervor, a very dangerous and volatile substance. There is little one can do to reason with those who proclaim they are driven by an invisible force. They qualify their actions by a divine right for a godly justice as opposed to man's justice. They become maniacs in a crowd of similar thinkers. A crowd inciting a riot who has lost individual reason: Mass hysteria could become suicidal behavior. Numbers that could overwhelm his men gain statistical strength.

With forceful hand movements Pontius gestures to his men to direct the prisoners to the edge of the wall.

Prodded by the soldiers, like a reluctant, broken-of-spirit, starved and beaten dog, Barabbas, bewildered and weak, limps to the edge. He is shoved by those who know no compassion, Acilius, Tarraco, Creticus, and Cicero. So tightly chained, a hasty step and he could trip and fall heavily on the hard-stone pavement. Dazed, undaunted, disconnected from the crowd, his eyes are cast down.

The crowd study him, and buzz among themselves. Some wonder who he is, and others whisper they think they recognize him but are unsure.

This ungainly, unbalanced entrance by Barabbas has the focus of the mob. The fine figure of physical fitness, Yeshua ha Mashiach, his Hebrew name, walks upright, unbound, naturally majestic, silent, with neither a perceptible arrogance nor superiority. He is different, hard to describe, a quiet charisma, majestic. Brilliant in a white robe of considerable worth, given to him by King Herod Antipas, this blameless man remains remarkably calm, hardly noticed, little seen. Yet some voices in the crowd begin to whisper his name as they know who he is yet they cower to defend him. He stands, motionless, flanked by a silent, uncomfortable, awe bound, Centurion Antonius. Outranked, Antonius in quiet reverent wonderment waits for Pontius to rescue this serene miracle worker who makes no claims and at times appears to be detached from his surroundings.

Seated as an unspoken sign of control, Pontius lounges back in his stone chair while the repugnant mob continues to chant "Barabbas." Pontius has the time, his initial impatience contained but the crowd begins agitating his perceived outward calm and momentary indifference. Militarily he has a time limit. The sound, rhythmic, sometimes discordant, others like instruments out of tune, add to the ominous atmosphere of an expectant mass in a minor motion on an ocean that could capsize his command.

Barabbas looks toward Yeshua without any awareness of his deity. But would Barabbas be the first to be saved? Yeshua, formerly popular with thousands, now suffers the indignity of being of less regard than the murderer who stands to his left. Despised by the Elite few, who tarnish the reputation of this quiet man, they plan to create such unrest; the numbers grow and may overwhelm the few hundred Roman soldiers. The Temple Guard lingers near Caiaphas. Any foreknowledge of what the outcome will be for this man who stands to the right of Barabbas, in the royal garment, completely eludes the dagger man. If he is still able to think at all, this fine man may be a collaborator too, which makes Yeshua treasonous to Barabbas and a danger to his brothers, the Sicarii.

Pontius rises, walks forward and pushes them apart and stands fearlessly between these two very different men. One broken man, a man whose violence has been returned upon him: The other man, still intact, complete with an uncanny sense of inner peace. The Prefect does not just glance at these two men on either side of him, he looks at them in such a way as to give them an opportunity. Pontius inwardly hopes the solution to the problem he now faces may be delivered by one of these men. Again, he surveys the growing numbers on the ground below him; restless pilgrims, a threat of insurrection, a faction that may incite a riot.

Pontius looks down from the wall, studies the gathering until his eyes pick out The High Priest Caiaphas. The man who previously engaged Pontius in a battle of wills that lasted six days now stands amongst his Temple peers and guards for protection, ready to once again resist the steel swords of Rome. With apparent unlimited resolve, Caiaphas is ready to enforce his own rule over that of Rome's representative. The atmosphere, like the intangible fire of a willful battle, heat rises. Some droplets of perspiration appear on the bare forehead of the Roman Prefect as he recalls the frustrations caused by his determined opponent. The adorned head of the Chief Priest, once again, stands his ground, held upright in the fine robes, embellished with gold embroidery, tassels, bells, all adding to his state of invincibility.

As the ordinary men in the crowd, drab in their earth tones, change perspective and follow the line-of-sight from Pontius high on the wall, they are uneasy at the sight of the colorful Roman soldiers who brandish their swords waiting for an order to defend their rule. The line takes their attention to Caiaphas. Some in the crowd see the contest before them. Others wait for the show to begin. Down in the masses, they grow silent again, they nudge, whisper among themselves. The Elite, the well-dressed, also know who Pontius looks disgustingly upon. It is not Barabbas. An eeriness returns.

Pontius senses the possible mounting opposition to his justice, but he tries to enforce his authority in an attempt to lead the crowd. He shouts at Caiaphas,

"Who do you want me to release to you? The King of the Yehudim?" [Mark 15:9 & John 18:39]

The voiceless mass waits like a slowly swirling sea of flotsam and jetsam. The Chief Priests pass the word to the people, that Pontius should release Barabbas. [Mark 15:11]

A scribe near Caiaphas, obviously under his influence, points at Yeshua…

"Crucify him!" [Mark 15:13]

… as to endear himself to the High Priest.

Pontius glares, determined not to give in to their demands.

They expect the High Priest to speak but he does not. Caiaphas looks around his tight circle that floats around him to find someone who will do his dirty bidding for him. He nods to another scribe who then points like a puppet and shrieks like a eunuch,

"Not this man but Barabbas!" [John 18:40]

Another lone voice squawks, "Crucify him!" [Mark 15:18] and the sound of the flies buzz more loudly.

With utter disdain the Prefect of Judea can hardly find any words to be a fit response to such a sickening statement. He glares. Caiaphas nods to let the whispering name slip from his slimy lips to his immediate stationary entourage, "Barabbas." The now overly familiar name ripples throughout the mob, bobbing from one to another, again aided by the Council Members, the Elite, the murmuring, nudging, whispering, pushing, shoving continues until the inevitable waterfall of sound pours out,

"Away with this man Yeshua, and release to us Barabbas." [Luke 23:18]

"Barabbas" the crowd roars.

Observer, calculator, adjudicator, Pontius, stands between the two men. Roman rule being denied on one side and local unrest, like a mounding dump, piles one piece of trash upon another.

"Release Barabbas, crucify Yeshua!" Pontius is astonished, "Why? What evil has he done?

I have found no crime deserving death." [Luke 23:22]

Without a second of justification, a lone voice comes out of the growing sea of refuse, "Crucify him! Crucify him!" [Luke 23:22]
Like water that finds its own level the sound of flies is oceanic, everywhere. As if to exasperate Pontius, the couplet ripples like the swell of the ocean around the mob. "Crucify him! Crucify him!" [Luke 23:22]

He turns to look at the two prisoners. He goes into action with frustration, anger and indignation. Summoning the by-standing soldiers, Acilius, Tarraco, Creticus, Cicero, he strips Barabbas of his manacles.

Barabbas is stunned, astonished, and faints. Incredulous, the murderer of the Elite comes alive. He cannot believe his good fortune. Then with silent anger Pontius shoves him forcibly toward the stairs. He trips and with renewed hope saves his fall as Pontius hastens his exit.

With cunning, using a legal technicality manipulated for their purposes, the Elite claim their right to release a prisoner, at their discretion, as part of the ritual this Passover. The order was concocted, Oral Laws to add to The Ten Commandments as a means to control the masses. Manipulating the authority of their God, they make it difficult for their humble subjects to be truly free of an oppression that Yeshua is sent to free them of. The reason these men of high standing are so against Yeshua can be fairly seen because he has come to defend those of low stance. This man neither benefits their political power, their material wealth, nor their control of the masses. Yeshua knows this. Pontius understands a little. The masses know nothing. The Elite dominate the mob to release the guilty in exchange for the death of the innocent.

The soldiers look equally surprised. Yeshua remains silent. All knowing he must endure his mission. But there is no jubilation from the mob either and their mumblings become mute. Another issue rests on this silence. The adjudication of the man who has done no harm: The good conscience of the crowd is being eroded. The forces of evil must be allowed to win this day. The New Covenant cannot be fulfilled without this transfer of the light of truth, into the darkness of lies first. Yeshua is the only person who knows his true destiny, his sacrifice for mankind.

Pontius contemplates who should take his order; he knows this to be against Antonius's principles. Pontius quietly says to Centurion Lefus, "Scourge him. Draw his blood so it may be seen, but not too much." But the ominous glints of pin like light within Centurion Lefus' dark eyes remain unnoticed by his commander. It would have been better had he given this order to Antonius who has a silenced respect for Yeshua. Pontius knows Antonius is sympathetic to Yeshua. He has momentarily forgotten that he told Antonius to keep quiet about this man. Antonius believes this majestic man healed his servant but lest the soldiers at the barracks lose their respect for this centurion, he has kept very quiet about it. Now the Prefect has placed Yeshua into the care of a sadistic man who enjoys seeing an easy victim fall under his control. The outcome may have been different than the travesty of justice about to take place had Antonius supervised the following miscarriage of justice. Pontius confirms for Antonius, "I will beat him and release him." [Luke 23:16]

The crowd strongly opposes the judgement, "Crucify him! Crucify him!" [Luke 23:21]

"Take Yeshua and scourge him," he also says to the Roman soldiers who stand-by. Acilius, Tarraco, Creticus, Cicero pull him away roughly.

The noise from below is a muddle of sounds that make up the phrase, "Crucify the blasphemer."

Lefus hears the order, "not too much," but he does not heed the caution. Lefus inwardly likes the prospect of some sport. Lefus follows Yeshua away with the directive to oversee the punishment.

This pleases Pontius, "I will beat him and let him go." [Luke 23:16] He has found the perfect solution. His justice will prevail in the end. Pontius has far from given into these callous, bullying, merciless, superstitious, cowards. Pontius will, he believes, be able to turn the minds of the restless crowd below him. The mob rumbles and mumbles and a lone voice boldly cries, "Crucify the blasphemer" Pontius ignores the sound, the buzz of flies.

Just a few days before when Pontius arrived in Jerusalem from Caesarea, this majestic man, Yeshua, was hailed as a prince. He has since learned that he was preceded into the city by Yeshua. Pontius himself was reminded he rode his horse over palms and blankets laid down before this man who was proclaimed a peacemaker, healer and teacher. The Prefect has been informed that this man has a group of loyal followers. But where are they now? He ponders, could they be in the crowd before him? Pontius also recalls a riot at the temple, an attack on the money-changers. Could this peaceful man be responsible or is it some made up charge to qualify the Elite's vehement intent to put him to death?

The morning sun grows in intensity as it rises in the sky. Pontius, at the edge of the wall, scans the crowd like a commander, and assesses his enemy. Only just within hearing range, the grunts of the soldiers, the lash of the whip, the silence of a torture so brutal it takes all the breath out of the victim. His troops at ground level stand attentively, alert and agitated. Lefus appears ahead of the scourged Yeshua.

"Look, I am bringing him out to you now, but I want you to know I find no fault in him!" [John 19.4] The mob roars in anticipation, an indefinable noise most similar to an amphitheater where sport has been the entertainment.

The white robe given to him by Herod Antipas has been replaced with a cheap, worn, purple, blood-soaked robe draped loosely over the shoulders of Yeshua. This exposes part of his back, red-raw, stripped of flesh, blood stains run down the backs to his legs and bare feet. Exhausted, brutalized, he can hardly stand. Pontius, wide-eyed, shocked at the sight of him, he glares disgusted at Lefus with a look that could sink a thousand Roman ships! Lefus shrugs it off.

The two women in the crowd, Mary Magdalene and Mary, mother of James, weep openly while looked upon coldly by those around them.

Pontius leads Yeshua gently by the arm to the edge of the wall. Yeshua staggers and flinches as Pontius turns him to reveal the tortured back of a once physically perfect man. Yeshua wears a crown of thorns: Blood trickles down his forehead from the thorns, over his eyes, down his nose, across his mouth. It is a sight that can be seen reflected on the face of the Prefect as great pity.

Another ripple and a waterfall of noise erupt from the crowd below. "Crucify him!"

Pontius screams "Just look at this man!" [John 19:5] Disgusted, he walks back to his desk and sits down until the mob quietens. The waterfall turns into the sound of swarming flies. He deliberates. Moments pass while Pontius listens to the buzz of the restless mob, it grows like flies around a corpse.

He stands, walks forward: He leans down over the wall to see angry faces. The cohort, 150 Roman soldiers, backs to the wall. The crowd jostles. He turns to his Centurion Antonius and nods at him to follow. "Bring up the other cohort."

Pontius, appalled, motions the four Roman soldiers, who guard Yeshua, to take Yeshua down the stairs. "And wait for me there!" He looks out over the crowd, pauses, walks to the edge of the wall and addresses them in a forced appeal. His manner he knows is better able to control them if he hides his emotions. "I bring him to you! Behold the man!" [John 19:14] with reverence and hope.

Caiaphas, devoid of humanity, coldly states his instruction to Pontius. "Crucify him, he breaks the law."

Pontius tries to ignore Caiaphas but he cannot. "Shall I crucify your king?" [John 19:15]

Caiaphas without a moment of hesitation rams back, "We have no king but Caesar." [John 19:15] Pontius descends the steps to ground level with renewed angry energy. He fully understands the hidden threat of being reported to Tiberius as a compliant. This appears to make Pontius guilty of losing control, thereby allowing a riot and a bloodbath, the result of letting one guilty blasphemer go free.

At the bottom of the stairs, in the stone courtyard, Pontius aggressively motions his soldiers with both hands to push Barabbas away. The buzz intensifies. Within the mob, Nicodemus and Joseph of Arimathea shake their heads, side-to-side, their mouths open, exclaim protestations which are not heard: "'Behold the man' whose name is The BRANCH."
[Zechariah 6:12]

The Mob joins in to drown him out, "Crucify him, crucify him."

Joseph of Arimathea's protest is unheard, "And he shall grow up out of his place."

Pontius grunts a deep sigh of frustration, outmaneuvered; he knows the Chief Priest and looks at Caiaphas with disdain and utter loathing.

"Away with him! Away With him! Crucify him, crucify him." [John 19:15] The ugly mob demands.

Pontius shouts toward Caiaphas, exasperated, defeated, "Take him for yourselves and crucify him for I find no crime in him." [John 19:6]

To torment Pontius, to submit to his demands, Caiaphas shouts back defiantly. "We have a law and by that law he ought to die because he has made himself the Son of Elohim." [John 19:7]

Pontius pauses, ever calculating, he looks out at the growing mob. He assesses the resistance. Then he looks again at Yeshua.

Increased size, noise, the voices in the Mob, and the words, "He has made himself the Son of Elohim," *terrifies* Pontius. [John 19:8] The Hebrew word "Elohim" for the God of the Israelites causes him to shudder to the core. Like any man confronted with the awesome magnificence of Holiness, the first reaction is fear mixed with unworthiness. He screams, "Bring him!"

Nicodemus and Joseph of Arimathea, mouths open, and their shouts, their protestations continue unheard. "… and he shall build the temple of YeHoVaH."

Pontius approaches Lefus. "Send a detachment north to meet the Tribune. Tell him to hurry."

He walks into the judgement hall and waits as the soldiers bring the injured, exhausted Yeshua. Impetuously Pontius approaches Yeshua. With personal intensity, "Where? Where are you from?" [John 19:9] Pontius stares at an unresponsive Yeshua. He pleads, borders upon begging, "Will you not speak to me? You refuse to speak to me? Don't you know I have the power to release you and the power to crucify you?" [John 19:10] Brutalized, injured, fatigued, weakly, Yeshua draws breath.

"You would have no power over me, unless it was given to you, from above." [John 19:11] Pontius looks skyward, moves in closely to listen to him. "Therefore, he who delivered me to you has the greater sin." [John 19:11] Pontius considers his position, registers his own desperation and fear, his inability to bring about justice. He sees before him a physically broken human being. The man faces a destiny. The mind of the Prefect, tormented by the events of the morning, has been rendered impotent as his thoughts jar at his conscience. The terror is not so much the noise of the mob, close to being out of control. His dread is this man before him knowingly has stated Pontius is not as sinful as those who have brought these false accusations. Pontius knows that to be correct. Yeshua remains silent.

Pontius motions his men to bring Yeshua outside. Pontius leads the way: His stride shows a rehearsed authority. He takes one last bite of this fight to right the wrong done to this meek man. Pontius walks out amongst the noisy crowd, points directions at his men.

A council member, a scribe, pushes his way next to the Prefect. "If you let this man go you are NOT Caesar's friend." [John 19:12] Then waits annoyingly in his personal space. The threat is clear. A contingent of the cohort pushes ahead of Pontius to open up the way for him. The scribe does not give up, "Whoever makes himself a king, speaks against Caesar." [John 19:12]

Yeshua stumbles forward slowly supported by the usual four soldiers tightly grouped. Pontius steps up on a raised stone platform boldly, his face white, drained of blood. The quiet crowd waits his next word.

Pontius utters forth with new belief. "Behold your king!" [John 19:15] He looks at Yeshua. The crowd roars disapprovals.

"Away with him! Away with him!" The roar dies down.

One lone voice exclaims again, "We have no king but Caesar." [John 19:15] The crowd roars approval. Pontius steps up on the platform raises his arms in the air and with stubborn indignation.

"Shall I crucify your king?" [John 19:15]

"Hail Caesar! Hail Caesar!" They blurt back to silence anything Pontius might say.

He steps off the platform to look closely into the eyes of Yeshua. Pontius's pleading stare at Yeshua one last time waits for an answer but Pontius knows he has lost. He looks into the cast down; the eyes of Yeshua are nearly closed. The Prefect momentarily casts his eyes down in shame not able to maintain eye contact. The burden of his office seems greater to him now than at any other time. All previous convictions and crucifixions were easy to dispatch. Succumbed to pressure he has failed this man. The crowd buzzes then deaf and silent: He again ascends the stone platform.

"We have no king but Caesar." [John 19:15] He knows that to be so very untrue. He knows they threaten him. Caiaphas has succeeded in stirring up the crowd against this man and against the Prefect too. Pontius wishes he had slain Caiaphas when he had the chance to do so. Now that act of mercy has come back to haunt this day. This far greater threat today than that day passed, has brought thousands of pilgrims into the city. Militarily and politically outmaneuvered he faces a single man who in and of himself presents no threat. But what if his supporters, who are absent today, should return and amass a force to contest these Elitists and their servants, to fight them for authority? They may do more harm than turn over tables in the temple. He has even heard a theory that they may destroy the temple in three days and then unbelievably rebuild it. He reverses himself, casts aside his panic that this man has come as their new king, as the Son of their Almighty, an idea that grips his soul with terror. But he has doubts about it all. His humanness cannot be denied. His carnal sense wrestles with his good conscience. Pontius turns to the nearest soldier.

"Fetch me some water. Before I am also falsely accused." [Matthew 27:24] He gazes at the restless and growing crowd and again with sorrow at the pathetic figure of the physically abused body of Yeshua. Once perfect, now a body torn to pieces by his men, a ridiculous crown of thorns still perched upon his head. Most of his blood appears outside instead of inside his body: Most of it darkly drying on the outside. He quietly stands in a way Pontius respects his serenity and his calmness. The soldier returns with a bowl of dirty water. Unheard against noise, the defeated administrator of justice proclaims, "I am innocent of the blood of this just person." [Matthew 27:24] Visibly disgusted he dips his hands in the bowl. "See to it yourselves" [Matthew 27:24] comes out of his mouth as angry revulsion. The water becomes clean. He looks for the non-existent towel to dry his hands.

An anonymous voice cries out, "His blood be on us and on our children." [Matthew 27:25] Without a thought for future implications that will be misread and misunderstood throughout the centuries. When in actuality this call for atonement is unwittingly stated. The covering of blood to cover the sins for all mankind as provided by this sacrifice of The Lamb of YeHoVaH. This Son of Man replaced the ceremonial sacrifice of the lambs of the land. But the majority in the crowd failed to understand this enactment of the New Covenant. This death is the will of YeHoVaH, not of the people who demanded it. Their sin is greater than that of Pontius.

In the crowd, Nicodemus and Joseph look to one another in shock. Joseph questions, "Why did Yeshua not defend himself?"

Nicodemus thoughtfully answers with reverence. "The prophet Isaiah told us, 'He is brought as a lamb to the slaughter, and as a sheep before his shearers are dumb, he opened not his mouth.'" [Isaiah 53:7]

He shakes his hands vigorously, and then wipes them dry in his garment. The crowd gets word: Rumbling murmurs decrease. Pontius descends the stone platform, walks away from Yeshua, ignores him, eyes down, angrily and briskly brushes aside anyone in his path. The soldiers follow behind. Yeshua, like the dead carcass of a lamb, is left surrounded by swarms of flies.

YESHUA

The Younger Pontius

Pontius "after & before"

Pontius "after"

Claudia

Antonius

Antonius in helmet

Angels collage

Herod Antipas

Gaius Caligula

Shira

13
DEATH

THE PLACE OF THE SKULL

The tortuous slow death on a wooden cross: The nails driven through the soft tissue of the wrists and between the heel bone and the legs with sadistic barbarism. Roman inhumanity brutalized the victim to experience pain in every single nerve and sinew of the complex human body. The humiliation, pinned, semi-naked, only very slightly elevated so the nailed feet are unable to make contact with the ground. The eyes of the accused and punished leveled with the line of-sight so passers-by may choose to stare, or heckle, or chant or ridicule. They may even strike out against the thief or the murderer, an opportunity for a victim or anyone else, to take out their own punishment upon the slowly dying, the condemned, and the helpless. This type of death may take three days before the naturally resilient human body slumps, succumbs to suffocation. The occupant of the cross, no longer able to raise his body to expand his diaphragm in his chest, prevents air to enter his chest cavity. His lungs become physically inoperable. The living pain unbearable; relief from life means a welcome death.

The Roman soldiers squat around Yeshua's fine robe, the one given to him by Herod Antipas. They cast lots to win the prize. Yeshua, naked, looks down upon them and says, "Father forgive them, for they know not what they do." [Luke 23:34]

THE ANTONIA FORTRESS

Pontius pushes through the vast crowds at the Antonia. Brisk, alone, he snarls as he pushes through any impediment to his progress. His indignation at being forced again to yield to the Yehudim has made him aggressive. He takes his horse from the stable, mounts, digs his heels in the flanks of the fine animal that neighs at the crowds. The stallion stamps his hooves into the dusty soil, raises his tail, excretes as he goes. Pontius hastens. The mob buzz like dirty black and green flies and part like The Red Sea to make way for the angry Roman. Once free to do so, he gallops as if he runs from his fate in hopes the exhilaration will lift the burden upon his mind. It does not.

HEROD'S PALACE

The murmurs among the kitchen staff at Herod's Palace confirm the fast-far-flung rumors that Yeshua has been condemned to death as a criminal. But it is true. Benjamin, the cook, and Shira confer about the injustice that this man, who was hailed as a peacemaker just one week before, should now be the subject of execution. Their astonishment is equaled by Claudia who looks pained as she becomes aware of another presence, the guilty judge whose sentence of death presses heavily upon his conscience.

Pontius enters briskly and a hush prevails to seize any possible movement. Angrily he looks around the kitchen. Stunned at his sudden appearance and his demeanor they all remain still and mute. Evidently, they can see he is on the verge of rage nothing the likes of which they have ever seen on this man before. In his hand he holds a flat square of wood. From the warm edge of the kitchen fire Pontius takes a cold piece of charcoal. He scans the room. They stand in awe. He shoves the wood and the gray marker to Shira.

"Write!" he shouts abruptly, "'Yeshua of Nazareth (Natzaret) King of the Jews,' in Hebrew." [Adapted John 19:19] Not knowing if she is literate, he notices her hesitancy; his voice goes up an octave to vocalize the word "Hebrew!" He waits for clarification. "Can you write Hebrew?" Adamant it must be in the language of the people.

Shira's eyes grow watery, she is shaken to the core with emotion. She cries from deep within. Claudia launches to defend Shira, "Don't upset Shira!" Claudia touches his arm, but he brushes it off. Shira takes the marker from Pontius while sobbing and shaking so much she cannot render the letters Y H V H. Blubbering through tears she splutters hesitatingly.

"Yeshua Ha'netzaeret V' melek Ha' Yehudim." Another breath takes her voice to an uncontrolled admission, tearfully, "Yeshua brought Lazarus back to life." As the words tumble out the last phrase becomes incomprehensible.

In frustrated rage, Pontius takes the marker and the blank square sign and hands it to Benjamin. His public persona now replaces his exposed private emotions:

"Can you write?" He pleads for someone to help him right the wrong and write the truth.

Benjamin takes it; his right hand "withered" - just four fingers, the middle two fingers fused, deformed thumb, carefully, awkwardly, slow in thought, renders the letters Y H

V H. Pontius watches the struggle of the 'withered' hand with a change to empathy.

He softens as he says, "I'll add the Latin and the Greek." [Adapted Luke 23:38 "Greek and Latin and Hebrew"]

Claudia comforts Shira. Pontius adds the inscriptions INRI [Adapted Luke 23:38 Latin] while everyone remains silent and watches. He gives the sign back to Benjamin, then changes his tone to command the cook, "Come with me."

Witness of many crucifixions, he has no desire to see another suffer the indignity. Outside the palace a slow flow of pedestrians passes. They stroll past the palace completely unaware of what has taken place. The condemnation of this unique man has gone unnoticed by thousands of pilgrims. Mus, silent as always, hands the reins of his horse to Pontius. He mounts, "Get up here" and pulls Benjamin onto the rump while Mus holds the bit to steady the stallion.

Heels to the flanks, the horse jerks forward. The cook, plaque in one-hand, grabs the Prefect's tunic just before he falls backwards off the hind quarters. Pontius pushes through the throngs of people in the streets. It may only be Good Providence that has prevented him from a collision with stalls and structures, or from trampling humans under hoof. His mission compels him to make amends.

THE ANTONIA FORTRESS

He stops abruptly outside the Antonia and pushes Benjamin off the horse. "Take the sign to Golgotha. It must be nailed up above *their* king." In this way the distance makes it easier for him. Pontius rides into the fortress. Benjamin holds the sign and scans the crowd as they move away north from the Antonia Fortress. The cook is bewildered, shaken with the idea. He has no desire to see a gruesome crucifixion.

Annas, the elderly chief priest, walks slowly toward him; Benjamin's choice becomes apparent. This man's position and respect is displayed with fashionable finery. Therefore, Benjamin believes this subject will do what the Roman Prefect wants him to do. He excitedly bursts forth and says, "The Prefect's orders: Nail it above Messiah's head." Benjamin pushes the sign at an indignant Annas.

Startled, Annas, says, "Wait." Benjamin stops. He stands and studies it for a moment. "Do not write, 'The King of the Jews' but 'This man *said* I am King of the Jews'". [John 19:21]

Suddenly and expectantly from the top of the wall, Pontius angrily booms down, red-faced.

"What I have written will remain written!" [John 19:22]

Annas looks up, hesitates, recognizes the fury on Pontius's face and then scurries away with the sign. Annas and his conspirators have won the day and got their wish, he sees no point in arguing further. Convinced or convicted, Pontius has put this announcement into history.

HEROD'S PALACE

The sun shines high in the sky approaching the midday hour. In the palace Pontius and Claudia eat wistfully and silently. Neither is able to discuss the morning's events or enjoy their refreshments. Their thoughts are consumed in solemn reflection. The 'atmospheric' noise of the pilgrim's chatter becomes fainter. Quietly they sit. Claudia studies her contemplative husband. Finally, Pontius pushes his plate of food away.

Outside the palace, passers-by look up. The sun grows dim from the circumference and closes slowly: "From bright to black as sackcloth and ashes." The Constellations, the Bull and the Ram appear in a southerly perspective. For this to happen at the midday hour, puts fear into the pilgrims who scurry nervously to wherever they were going.

Inside the palace, the room is gray-black. Pontius gets up from the lunch table to look out. Darkness has fallen. He stumbles. "Darkness at this hour?"

Claudia, fearful, moves, to be alongside him: She remarks with incredulity in her voice. "Stars shine at day?"

They walk outside onto a veranda. In the distance, thunder: He puts his arm around her. The skies are star-filled as if night. No rain falls. Claudia, worried, studies Pontius. An imperceptive impulse gives way to an exclamation. "The Rabbi!" she says with certainty. Intuitively she knows thunder to be the voice of YeHoVaH. Her husband looks at her quizzically.

Constellations appear in a northerly perspective, Libre, Big and Little Dipper, The Bears, and the Full Moon glows as red as blood. Pontius says, "Impossible."

Claudia with imaginative, intuitive thought says quietly, "He commands the sun, the moon and the stars." A light appears; a lantern, carried by Antonius, exits the room to join them on the veranda. It illuminates their awestruck faces.

In a calm heightened state of awareness Antonius makes his heartfelt request known. "May I go to the crucified Rabbi?"

Pontius studies him for a moment. "This Rabbi, was he the same one who healed your servant?"

"Yes."

Claudia believes her husband realized that although he would prefer to deny it and so she tells him so. "You knew."

Pontius ignores her, shakes his head and with guilt asks Antonius, "Why did you not speak up?"

Antonius looks at Claudia and before he can speak, she says, "You told him not to!"

He covers the past immediately and gives Antonius his permission.

"Yes. Go. Report back!"

Antonius leaves. Pontius, lamentably, stares at Claudia. She looks up into the stars and sky. The stars sparkle against the night sky and the blood moon gives just enough light to show the eerie quiet presence of those who wander down the streets. This blackout lasts three hours.

THE PLACE OF THE SKULL

Goliath's head is buried in Golgotha. As the third hour of darkness comes closer to the fourth hour, a few quietly 'lost' people gather. Citizens and soldiers look up to the sky, mystified. Two women kneel at the feet, at the base of the middle cross where Yeshua hangs in silence, his back to the rock and his face in blackness. The two named Mary, sob. The two thieves on either side of Yeshua, suffer the same painful punishment, in subdued groans and moans, both fade in and out of consciousness.

Centurion Antonius approaches, bends down, reaches around the women and touches the blood that trickles down the base of the cross. A woman's hand touches the bloody impaled feet in compassion. They make a symbolic claim because they do not know the Roman. Antonius watches the blood flow into the rock at the base of the cross.

THE TEMPLE

The sliced throat of a lamb bleeds onto the solid Rock of Sacrifice in Solomon's Temple. Caiaphas states, "It is finished." With knife in hand, Caiaphas stands up. He looks down at his feet as he feels something move underfoot.

In darkness, within the Inner Temple, an earthquake's ominous rumble shakes a stone lintel above a vast woven curtain; sixty feet high, thirty feet wide; made of seventy-two squares of scarlet, blue, white and purple. Latitudinal, from right to left, the curtain stretches; from the top, the threads pop and break, a tear begins and rips vertically with great force and a great tearing sound.

The voice of Yeshua heard from Golgotha cries, "It is finished." [John 19:30]

The curtain opens from top to bottom giving access to the Holy of Holies, where only priests are allowed, more stones fall: The stone lintel, above, dislodges, breaks, splinters like shards of glass, and crashes to the ground in a cloud of dust. (The Son of Man, Yeshua, gives everyone the access to The Holy Father YeHoVaH.)

The rumble of the earthquake quietens for a moment. Distant sounds of cheers and merriment react to the spectacular sunrise in the sky as the aperture of light opens the second dawn of a very different day.

A CAVE

Before the fourth hour begins, the sunlight returns, and shines through the cracks in the rock. The violence of the earthquake splits boulders, rock faces, and makes cliff edges crumble. A sarcophagus, like a large stone coffin, shakes, dislodges some twenty feet below ground.

Cracks of light appear. The rays illuminate the cave sufficiently to reveal inside the sarcophagus, a chest, an expanse of gold, with the gold wings of two angelic figurines which form arm rests and back rests. Blood puddles on this seat. Blood mixed with water splashes. Through open cracks in the rocks the flow continues. Pink liquid forms on the ceiling inside this hewn-out cave.

Far from being what it was, ever again, this day will go down in the annals of history to intrigue the curious and confound the scientific.

THE PLACE OF THE SKULL

Body fluid and blood trickles from a spear wound in the side of Yeshua who hangs motionless on the middle cross. Antonius quietly mumbles, "Truly this man was The Son of YeHoVaH." [Mark 15:39] The blood and water flow through an open crack in the base stone, an indent that holds the cross. The ground shakes again as if the whole of the earth grieves this dead man.

A face familiar to Antonius, the Sanhedrin member, Joseph of Arimathea, approaches. They engage in conversation and walk away together. An incongruity of their stations in life, one Roman, one Hebrew, but both have something very much in common and it is not of this earthly realm.

HEROD'S PALACE

Claudia, evidently excitedly, relieved, looks to her husband for a change in his troubled state. Pontius blows out the redundant lantern. As he begins to adjust, believing all has returned to normal, the floor beneath his feet quivers. In full daylight it is difficult to decide what is more fearful, an earthquake during the dark hours when nothing can be clearly determined, or now, when every crack and speck of dust is visible. Alarm returns: Claudia feels the shake too; their moment of reprieve has ended. As dust starts to fall the earthquake takes on a voice of its own. Screams can be heard in the distance. The table shakes violently; the flame-less lantern falls over. Pontius takes Claudia by the hand to exit hurriedly.

They view the city from their balcony. Rocks rise out of the ground to the surface. Claudia and Pontius look astonished. Claudia says, "See that?" The shaking unnerves them. They descend to ground level quickly. Roman guards of the household appear.

In disbelief Pontius asks Claudia, "See what???" She clings to him as he proceeds, followed by soldiers. They watch the people run hither and dither, some of whom mumble indecipherable chatter. The land lies down; a loose stone falls; the exposed rocks still. Claudia, Pontius and the soldiers look around; calmness returns momentarily.

THE PLACE OF THE SKULL

The three crucifixions line the rock face of Golgotha. Another earthquake: Hundreds of people run in fear. The small rocks spill over the entrances to the natural caves and shower down. Boulders split, noise rumbles, and cracks increase. The ground heaves, and opens in various areas near grave sites. Large stones that close the tomb doors crack wide open with an explosive bang! People scream and run.

THE PALACE

Joseph of Arimathea holds a linen shroud as he stands alone outside the palace. People hurriedly pass by in a frenzy, afraid to stop lest the bowels of the earth swallow them whole. They are in contrast to Joseph's calmness. He watches them run towards nothingness.

Inside the palace Pontius and Claudia sit. Shira stands by to await her instructions. Antonius walks in to tell Pontius, "A member of the Sanhedrin waits outside to speak to you about Yeshua Ha Mashiach." Claudia stands up and eagerly walks ahead. Shira looks to the handsome Antonius hoping for his attention and receives a sideways glance.

"Huh. Another one who will not come in, yet I must go out to him." Pontius says.

Antonius replies, "This man is the honorable Yehudi, Joseph of Arimathea."

Shira notes the calm affinity he has with his words and smiles.

Pontius stands. "These people make no sense to me. Come." He relents because the day's events intrigue him, and he knows inwardly Antonius is correct about this man. Unlike the unreasonable men who forced Pontius's hand to execute Yeshua, this member of the Sanhedrin has his respect. Pontius follows the lead of Claudia and Antonius trails behind them. Lefus enters and moves upon Shira directly.

Outside the palace, Pontius and Claudia and Antonius approach Joseph of Arimathea who holds the linen shroud. Claudia examines the material while Joseph's question is a polite request, "I have come to ask your permission, for the body of Yeshua." [Adapted Luke 23:52 Mark 15:43 & John 19:38] Claudia looks to her husband and pointedly to Joseph of Arimathea.

"Death in this manner takes a long time," Pontius says with an anticipatory surprise in his voice. [Adapted Mark 15:44] Antonius is quick to confirm Yeshua is dead. Pontius now looks remarkably taken aback. "His legs were broken to hasten his death?" [Adapted John 19:31]

Antonius answers, "No. One of the guards thrust a spear in his side. The water ran. He was already dead." [Adapted John 19:33] Pontius turns back to Joseph.

Joseph presses on, "I wish to bury him." Pontius notices the alliance between Antonius and Joseph. Antonius looks at Joseph and then back to Pontius.

"Huh. You can have him." This subject remains as an irritant under his skin. Without delay or hardly a nod of thanks, Joseph departs. Pontius nods at Antonius who follows Joseph. Pontius and Claudia walk back into the palace passing a red-faced, disgruntled Lefus who strides out.

Claudia turns on her husband. "How can you be so detached?"

Pontius looks surprised and defensive. "Are you and your cousin Roman?"

Pontius harbors some of the guilt of Yeshua's death as much as he tries to deflect the blame on others. He has to live with his own disbelief, skeptical also about what has actually taken place, the unnatural, natural events, yet his curiosity prevails. He has become changed mysteriously but he internalizes questions of doubt rather than accepting his own conscience, an intuitive knowledge of the deity of Yeshua, YeHoVaH in the personage of a human being.

Shira avoided the advances of Lefus, and now straightens the furniture, and remains silent on all matters. She knows Yeshua. She intuitively senses danger from Lefus, who smolders.

14
THEFT

HEROD'S PALACE

Members of The Hebrew Council stand outside the palace the next day, Thursday, April 29th 28 CE [The Chronological Gospels Page 258] before a bored and impatient Pontius who yawns. The Chief Priest Caiaphas, "Sir, that imposter said, while still alive, 'After three days I will rise again.' [Matthew 27:63] Therefore make an order to secure the tomb until the third day, to prevent his disciples from stealing the body." Centurions Lefus and Antonius stand-by with Claudia to observe.

Pontius discovers a newly found longsuffering side to himself, remarkably patient he considers the toilsome nature of the Chief Priest. To withstand the assaults of this man who holds himself so very high, so very mighty, to be single minded in all that he does, Pontius takes his time. He becomes tolerant of this man who has pitched himself against Roman rule, piled up insults, threatened him, brought an innocent man to trial and forced him to be condemned. How long will his newfound patience last?

Pontius begins to pace back and forth, troubled by a new topic that drains his endurance. The High Priest comes with his onslaught of arrogant demands ordered in such a way as to surely ignite a fire in the Prefect. Careful to not meet fire with fire, Pontius restrains himself, and remains the listener. Annas fills this gap in the conversation. "They would tell the people 'he has risen from the dead' and this last fraudulent act would be worse than the first lie." [Matthew 27:64]

Pontius struts weary of the situation, but tolerant. He eyes both men and allows them time to unload all their demands and ideas so he can build-up his defenses and counter their arguments. The Prefect knows he must gain emotional intelligence to refrain from impulsive decisions. Caiaphas offers a token for manipulative compliance. "I will send my Temple Officers and Guards and you, shall send, --- how many?"

Pontius stops and looks Caiaphas straight in his eyes, and seethes with measured restraint about to blow the top off a steaming cauldron.

"This man Yeshua gave his life away. Indefensibly! You incited the crowd to near riot. You threaten me?" Do you think I do not know these things? Huh?"

Caiaphas backs down. Pontius turns on Annas next. The lid flies off.

"I put a suspected insurrectionist to death at your demand!" Without a break he lowers his voice to a quiet theatrical whisper. 'Now you tell me' He says as he pauses to make them think they have spoken a secret, 'that if his dead body is stolen ...' he walks over to a table and reignites in a burst of flaming intensity, neck veins protruding, his face turns burgundy, 'this is worse than if he were made alive again!'" Righteous indignation has won him over.

Claudia looks concerned for her husband.

Lefus and Antonius know when not to speak.

Pontius glares at Caiaphas. He then looks down at the table upon which rests the aqueduct model as if to consider his next verbal slaughter upon these two despicable men of self-importance and arrogant pride. In their positions, this human trait impatience resurfaces with fury. For the first time Caiaphas and Annas appear fearful in the company of the raging Roman ruler. Pontius considers all the ramifications of these two troublesome leaders, and all the possible unfavorable reports that might be made to Tiberius Caesar, he again moderates, reasons with himself, and reverses. He has expelled the truth, now he must address this new fantasy.

"Antonius. Tell the Ingeniare to secure the tomb as if it were the aqueduct! Go!" He looks at Annas with distain and in a guttural tone utters. "Such foolishness."

Pontius turns on Caiaphas knowing this man's games are played to win. For all his posturing of impatience the Prefect knows he must bide his time. He will let the course of events flow until a body of political liquid carries away The Chief Priest. He becomes swept along with buoyancy that must take all possible blame down current from Pontius. At least that is his hope.

"You always get your way. And you will."

The evening of the same day, the day after the crucifixion, Pontius carefully instructs his men to secure the stone door to the tomb to make it impossible to break-in. He affirms it with Antonius, plus three soldiers and the Ingeniare leave with paraphernalia and engineering tools.

THE TOMB

Like a huge two-ton grinding wheel on edge, a rolled rock-door, in a downhill sloped cut-out of a trough, closes the entrance to the tomb making it impenetrable. "Thud." The Ingeniare dips a long iron rod into a pot of hot bubbling molten lead over a small fire. Through bedrock, there is a drilled hole in the top right side of the huge round stone that conceals the entrance to the tomb. Holding tongs, he hammers the lead covered rod. Joseph of Arimathea, the owner of the tomb, stands aside. Annas inspects the work. The Ingeniare shakes his head at Annas in disbelief, gathers his tools and leaves with Antonius.

Three Roman soldiers stand with their backs to the stone. Another twenty-seven soldiers arrive, gather around, find suitable resting places, and sit down for the night. One soldier builds a campfire. Annas and members of The Council ignore Joseph of Arimathea who observes Antonius and the Ingeniare take leave.

A small contingent of Temple Guards arrive to take up positions near the entrance to the tomb. They do not acknowledge the Roman soldiers and keep close to themselves. Annas and the Council approach the Temple Guards to point out the secure Roman seal that has been fixed to the tomb door and through into the bedrock. Nothing could possibly break the 'lock' on that door. Satisfied, Annas and the Council leave.

HEBREW KITCHEN

The next day, now two days after the crucifixion, two women prepare burial spices and ointments before sunset on

Friday. Mary the mother of Yeshua and Mary, a friend, who has stood by Mary for the whole ordeal, wrap the bundle in a cloth.

THE TOMB

A total of three nights has passed since the crucifixion. Saturday morning, May 1st 28 CE [The Chronological Gospels Page 259] inside the pitch blackness of space, in the tomb that belongs to Joseph of Arimathea, the form of a human head and shoulders, torso and legs, lies motionless under a linen shroud. The form glows ever so slightly to define the shape. The walls of the rock tomb become visible and the roof of the cave takes on a soft light. The florescence of the form gradually becomes brighter until the skeleton is visible, like an x-ray, through the linen cloth. The intensity of the light increases and obliterates the shapes as the body metamorphoses into pure and brilliant light. Atoms reform as light moves from below, through the shroud, to above. At a levitated state above the shroud, above the rock ledge, the atoms reshape the human form*. The napkin that wraps around the top of the head and under the chin falls away gently.

*Known as ANTHROPOMORPHISM, when the form of a human changes, or "man change." Angels sent by YeHoVaH also go through this process when they become human.

The horizontal body becomes vertical and simultaneously lowers to the ground until the feet make contact. The lungs inhale deeply to begin breathing again, the eyes open, the mouth opens slightly.

The wound on His side made by the Roman spear has dried and healed to leave a big scar. The multi-numerous lacerations on his back have also dried as rough raised scars. In his wrists the holes from the nails that have caused damage to the bones and tendons have practically regrown, closed wounds but remain as small open channels. The many small lacerations across his forehead show where the thorns deeply pricked the thin skin and raised scars. Both his heels are pierced but now provide the support for his weight without impairment. His body remains in a state of cool light. Wearing only a cloth to cover his lower abdomen and posterior his legs begin to carry him toward the closed rock door of the tomb. Suddenly his body metamorphoses as pure and brilliant light again and continues to move through the dense rock. He leaves the tomb in a state of pitch blackness.

The gray night light of the outside world penetrates in a split second by lightening without crack or thunder. The flash is too fast to be recognized by the human eyes of the soldiers and Temple Guards that are present. The whole solid form including His head, the back of Yeshua's shoulders, torso and legs, walks away from the tomb. He wears a light-colored robe. He passes three soldiers, moves beyond the twenty-seven men but none of them apprehend Him. They stand, sit, faint and relax, sleep, around burning fires: None of their eyes follow a line-of-sight to Yeshua. They see nothing. Yeshua continues to move away and through the group of Temple Guards who are oblivious. He passes peacefully behind one Temple Guard, who stirs, flinches, immediately twists around to see nothing, gently collapses in the process. None of them see Him! He disappears.

THE BARLEY FIELD

In the failing light after sunset, a field full of barley, yet to be harvested, near the Mount of Olives, gazed upon by a group of farmers. Ten standing shocks of aviv barley, bound together, in the foreground, the Temple in the background. The farmers stand around until they are sure the Sabbath has ended. A few of them separate from the others to gather up the standing shocks of barley. They set off toward the city to deliver these first fruits to the Priest.

THE PALACE

At the palace, Claudia and Pontius play an ancient board game. Claudia has the upper hand. She laughs. A tremor causes the game pieces to shake violently. Suddenly Claudia looks fearful. Pontius reassures her, "An aftershock." Claudia grabs his hand in fright. Another tremor: Claudia grabs him with two hands! Pontius again, "Earthquakes occur in close succession." She 'throws' his hands away.

Her husband has sent The Rabbi to his death. A very destructive earthquake comes to disharmonize their home. Claudia expresses her panic, "We should be in Caesarea!"

"So, am I to blame?"

"You always have a practical answer for everything!" The ambiguity of her statement could be humorous but the ground shakes and astonishment registers again.

He shakes his arms and shoulders. "For this too?" he says testily.

OUTSIDE THE CITY OF JERUSALEM

Tombs and graves open. The dead rise and begin to walk. [Adapted Matthew 27:52.53] In the streets leading to the city hundreds of people stand aghast, as they see the dead walk. Some can be identified by the burial clothes wrapped around them. The farmers carry the shocks of barley, mingle with the living and the once dead. The crowds stunned speechless. The farmers pick up in haste to the Temple.

THE TEMPLE

The damage, evidence of the earthquake remains. Dust, rocks, the broken lintel and rubble pushed to one side. The huge rent veil folded and pushed to the other side. Ragged sheets and cloths hang were the majestic curtain once hung to obscure the view into The Holy of Hollies.

Caiaphas stands at the alter ready to receive the barley as the farmers rush toward him he grows more perplexed at their seeming lack of respect.

"You are in YeHoVaH's sanctuary."

"We saw the dead walk!" The farmers clamor to nod affirmations to push in on The Chief Priest's space.

Caiaphas takes the barley from them.

"It's true. It's true the dead have left their graves" one of the excited farmers proclaims with madness in his eyes.

Caiaphas, with the barley in hand, steps back from these crazy men and places it at the altar. Incensed at this ridiculousness, "Stop! You had too much wine! How dare you come here in this condition." He looks to one of the farmers. "You! Yes you! Begin the story of the offering and the blessings of YeHoVaH now and stop this nonsense!"

THE PLACE OF THE SKULL

At the garden tomb a huge, two-foot thick, stone disc, thirteen feet in diameter, stands vertical on edge, and covers the entrance of the now empty tomb. Three Roman soldiers stand with their backs to the sealed entrance unaware that Yeshua left the day before.

Before sunrise, Sunday, May 2nd, 28 CE [The Chronological Gospels Page 261]: the ground shakes: The guards look down at their feet. Driven into the rock, on the top right is the Roman seal; the iron rod sunk in lead now quivers under pressure. The soldiers are drawn to look at it.

The ground below the stone shakes more violently. The stone disc grinds but the rod prevents the stone from moving! Another great shudder comes. Another earthquake!

From on top of the tomb his countenance like lightening, his garments white as snow, and the angel creature appears. [Matthew 28:3 Mark 9:3] The many Roman soldiers, gathered, look at one another with intense fear. They become speechless unable to communicate with the apparition that also paralyzes their blank minds of any curiosity they may have.

Light touches the rock, hits on the iron rod, and the huge round stone begins to creak. It crunches, grinds, and dislodges slightly. The three Roman soldiers, Acilius, Tarraco and Creticus turn around, blinded by the light. Floodlit, now the whole rock violently shakes back and forth, half-an-inch at a time. Temple Guards, about five, take note, stand up at the periphery of the Roman group and mumble nonsensically. The campfire throws small embers up into the air.

The ground shudders and shakes again: The huge round stone presses at the iron rod, grinds, moves. An enormous, localized, explosive quake: Like lightening-crack-bang! The iron rod snaps cleanly! The round stone rolls slowly uphill, forces unseen, crunches and grinds and stops. Spot lit, as if moved by the light itself, a stone chock lodges at the base. The huge round stone grinds against the chock, a screeching sound. The entrance to the tomb, now open: dark and empty inside. The Roman Soldiers and Temple Guards shake with fear and fall down on the spot as dead men. [Matthew 28:4]

While still dark in the early hours of the morning at the tomb, in stark contrast to before, the Temple Guards and Roman soldiers have all deserted. The embers smolder, the campfire left to die away. The angel has disappeared: The tomb remains open.

Two women, Mary Magdalene and Mary, mother of James and Yeshua, carry the cloth that wraps the spices and oils. The two Women approach the entrance to the tomb; stop and stare wide-eyed. Sitting on the top of the stone, his face shines like lightning and his clothing as white as snow, the angel has returned anthropomorphically.

"Don't be afraid. I know you are looking for Yeshua, who was crucified. He is not here! He is raised from the dead, just as He said would happen. Come; see where his body was lying." [Matthew 28:6 Mark 16:6]

Mary Magdalene and Mary tremble with excitement and enter the tomb at once. They look around in wonderment. The burial shroud remains untouched where it fell flat on the stone base. The napkin neatly folded. The two women drop their spices and oil, exit, thrilled at their discovery: The angel speaks with a warm and kindly authority.

"And now, go quickly and tell his disciples that He has risen from the dead. And He is going ahead of you to Galilee. You will see Him there. Remember what I have told you."
[Matthew 28:7 Mark 16:7]

They leave in quiet awe, renewed with hope.

Two of the disciples, Yachanan (John) and Kefa (Peter), run toward the tomb: Yachanan outruns Kefa to reach the entrance first and stops. Yachanan stoops down, looks in to see the shroud as it lays in place flat upon the stone slab. The napkin neatly folded, set apart, appears on the ground some distance from the linen shroud. Spices and oils abound. Kefa boldly walks past Yachanan and enters the tomb. Kefa 'mimes' the distance by paces, steps between the folded napkin and the shroud, to measure the distance as if to imitate Yeshua. Yachanan walks in to see the shroud lays flat exactly in a place where the body would have laid. They look at each other happily bewildered and walk away quickly.

JERUSALEM

In Jerusalem some thirty Romans and five Temple Guards approach the home of Annas. One steps forward as Annas faces them: "The tomb that belongs to the Sanhedrin member, Joseph of Arimathea..."

Annas looks at the large gathering too many for him to accommodate in private and too public to continue. "Let us not talk here. Come with me, all of you."

CAIAPHAS'S PALACE

They huddle into the palace that belongs to Caiaphas. The Council looks on while Caiaphas focuses intently.

Annas points to the soldier who speaks for them. "Tell us, Yeshua's body has gone."

"They will say we fell asleep on duty."

Another soldier picks up the anxiety. "Under Roman law, we will be executed."

Caiaphas looks around those assembled who wait for him to offer up an explanation.

"That will be our death sentence!"

Caiaphas leaves while the Romans anxiously and noisily babble among themselves. The Temple Guards, not under the threat of execution remain silent.

Caiaphas returns to deposit many small pouches with the Elders of The Council. [Matthew 28:12]

"You must say, 'His disciples came by night and stole him away while we were asleep.'" [Matthew 28:13]

"This is for your defense. For each and every one of you." Caiaphas directs the Elders to pass the pouches of coins to each and every soldier. "And if it comes to the Prefect's ears, we will satisfy him also." [Matthew 28:14]

The soldiers look to one another for solace; none comes. The "defense fund" does not change their guilt. For all of them to be asleep on watch hardly sounds realistic. Would they all be asleep at the same time? The fact they cannot give a reasonable explanation would expose them as accomplices. Their cooperation with the thieves who stole the body of Yeshua places them in serious jeopardy.

THE PLACE OF THE SKULL

Amazed at this, Pontius hastens to the scene to examine the stone door of the tomb. Four Roman soldiers have returned to duty as lookouts. Pontius and the Ingeniare stand and examine the damage to the stone around the iron rod. There is none, just a clean break. Pontius examines the stone channel at ground level. Being familiar with the construction of aqueducts he looks closely at the slight incline.

Pontius says incredulously, "That stone rolled uphill?"

The Ingeniare shakes his head in disbelief. Claudia and Antonius approach the tomb, look inside and then enter: The myrrh, aloes, spices and fragrances have all gone, as has the burial shroud and napkin.

Pontius is confounded by what he sees. "You are the Ingeniare!" Pontius rubs his finger on the broken iron rod. "How?"

The Ingeniare answer, "It is impossible for the rod to shear off so cleanly."

"The force?" asks Pontius.

"The earthquake," the Ingeniare theorizes, "should have done more damage to the stone."

Pontius points down at the stop-chock. "Someone had to put that there."

Claudia emerges from the dark to pick up on the conversation. "Could the stone be rolled from the inside?"

Pontius looks at his wife in disbelief. Antonius starts first with a smile. Pontius begins to laugh. The Ingeniare joins in and points to the stop-chock that is on the outside of the tomb. Claudia finally sees the funny side. While indeed mysterious there seems to be an atmosphere of some relief that the innocent man has disappeared. The evidence of the extreme brutalization that Yeshua suffered has also gone from this place. Any blood that may have dripped from the body to the stone base has gone. Pontius feels a strange temporary relief. They all sense the new atmosphere that permeates their being with an uncanny peace.

THE FORTRESS

Pontius sits at a table in the Antonia Fortress. Centurion Lefus, Caiaphas and members of the Council enter. Lefus stands to one side. Caiaphas puts a large pouch of coins on the desk.

"Ah! And this is the reward for the return of the stolen body?" Pontius assumes.

"Followers of Yeshua will make false claims. He has come back to life to start a revolution." Caiaphas says with his usual surety.

Standing slowly, thinking, Pontius takes the pouch of coins and as he hands it back to Caiaphas says, "No wonder you need your YeHoVaH to come to your aid. Listen to yourselves. Huh. If I do not put the Rabbi to death, he causes a revolution. Prevent the theft of the body, guard it, and stop a revolution. Now the Rabbi is dead, the body stolen, so a rebellion is inevitable, is it?"

Caiaphas says, "If we work together, we can prevent this. To execute your men ..." Pontius frowns. "...brings validity to the claim that Yeshua's body was stolen away or speculation that claims the carpenter is still alive. It's preposterous. You and I know this but his followers are gullible. Let's keep this a private matter." Caiaphas places the pouch back on the table and pushes it toward Pontius.

"Everyone knows!" Pontius takes the pouch and juggles with it. "Your Temple Guards and my soldiers will have told everyone by now. The God of your Yehudim made them all fall down like dead men."

Pontius ruminates with an idea that would have been preferable. The longsuffering patience he has held toward Caiaphas leaves him now as anger returns.

"I should have had your neck when you presented it to me."

He throws the pouch back at Caiaphas who jumps nervously as he catches it. Dominicus comes briefly to his mind when she threw a pouch of coins at him. "You will need that money to pay the taxes for the new aqueduct." He impatiently and angrily dismisses him, shakes his sweeping fore hands at Caiaphas and his entourage. They refuse.

"Lefus. Escort them out!"

Lefus does not approve of the Prefect's restraint. He hopes Pontius will become the aggressor. He does not understand politics, only force. Insubordinate, resistant, Lefus bodily pushes them out with the palms of his hands. "Move along, move along."

15

SEARCH

Joseph of Arimathea, flanked by two Roman soldiers hurry along the streets of Jerusalem.

THE ANTONIA FORTRESS

The Antonia Fortress has an aura of foreboding doom for all the men. In particular, the three Roman soldiers, Acilius, Tarraco and Creticus, who brutally flagellated Yeshua look aghast, incredulous at their arresting officer, the Tribune. A tall, stern-faced man sent by the Legate of Syria, walks up to the same three who guarded the tomb, and orders Centurion Lefus to push them into the building.

Lefus and the two Roman Soldiers enter with Joseph of Arimathea. Pontius sits behind the table upon which rests a large dagger, the type used by the Sicarii. His demeanor so serious, this small room in the fortress perpetuates his mood of morbidity. Pontius waves at the soldiers; dismissive: They exit.

Pontius asks a peaceful unshakable Joseph very abruptly "Do you know why I have summoned you here today?"

"I am implicated in the disappearance of the Messiah."

"Hum. 'The Messiah?' You are the chief suspect." Pontius rises from the table.

"Prefect: To start your investigation with me is logical and therefore correct."

Pontius takes the dagger in his hand with thoughts he might have to take Joseph by surprise to dislodge the information he requires.

"And this belonged to?"

Joseph shakes his head negatively, ignores the knife, "His miracles, he healed the sick, called forth a man from the dead, to defy our human logic."

Pontius begins to pace. An attempt to explain the extra ordinary events of recent times goes beyond the pragmatism of the Prefect. An exercise in futility as Joseph discerns in the spirit Pontius as one who resists knowing the truth. Even though he was confronted by Yeshua who told him He was the personification of truth. Joseph knows many were called but few heard.

"Why would the crowd call for the release of a known murderer, Barabbas, a murderer of wealthy Yehudim like you?"

"Would it be reasonable to assume there were enough supporters of Barabbas to intimidate the crowd?" Joseph allows that to sink in for a brief moment. "The real conflict here is the general populace may support those who would murder the wealthy, those who profit from the poor."

Continuing to pace back and forth, intrigued by the suggestion, Pontius listens, waits for more.

"Barabbas killed those who he perceived as profiteers." He waits another moment to take note that Pontius is receptive to hear more. "The noble wealthy men he killed, regardless of their affiliation with Rome, whether you knew them or not, well perhaps his genocide he thought would destabilize your Roman rule and then mount an insurrection. Perhaps that was his plan."

Pontius ponders the sound logic of this learned man.

"You are saying the poor people liked Barabbas" and then Pontius switches the topic quickly.

"Perhaps. Who do you think stole the body of Yeshua?"

Joseph exudes something intangible. Secure in his demeanor, a grounded anchor, a tone of truth that the Prefect feels compelled to shake to keep on course. Joseph ignores the question and strikes at truth. "The Psalms state, 'They have pierced my hands and feet'. He is the sacrifice, to atone for us." [Psalm 22:16]

Pontius looks intently at Joseph. "A sacrifice?"

To regain control of the interview, he suddenly places the sharp tip of the dagger under Joseph's chin. Unflinching, Joseph raises his head higher.

"Who did you collaborate with to steal the body of this man so that his followers could say he has risen from the dead?"

Joseph retaliates quickly with more logic. "Do you think I could *overpower* your men while they stood guard?"

"You drugged them with a sleeping potion!"

"How could this benefit me?"

Pontius slowly relaxes his grip. He puts the dagger back on the table.

"You are guilty, because you had the opportunity."

Joseph studies Pontius for a moment. Each stare down the other.

"It was predestined, His destiny." Joseph says and hits a nerve. Pontius holds to his own secret guilt for allowing the miscarriage of justice. What Joseph has said makes it even more difficult to comprehend the meaning of it all. Like any man who denies the deity of The Messiah he will become steadfast in his own disbelief. He knows his actions and his alone resulted in the death of the innocent man from Galilee. Therefore, Pontius is not likely to forgive himself his own failure. Impatience reigns forth from Pontius, again.

"You remain under suspicion; until the body is returned."

In his defense Joseph insists, "Your Ingeniare sealed that tomb with an iron rod."

Pontius sits down at the table. He concedes and nods all knowingly at Joseph.

"Lefus! Go find the Tribune and bring him here."

Joseph pushes his point with logic, "No man could break that iron seal."

"Well, someone did!"

In the courtyard the Tribune faces the group of thirty soldiers who guarded the tomb.
The straight line-up separates them distinctly from the others. In the periphery an even larger number of soldiers watch the proceedings. The most vocal of the soldiers speaks up for his defense.

He is one of the three, Acilius.

"A lightening force so strong we were thrown to the ground."

The Tribune eyes Acilius and says, "The court will be lenient."

Lefus brings Joseph of Arimathea to look upon justice, Roman style. The Tribune moves to the beginning of the line, pauses and starts to count, walks further from left to right not making eye contact.

"1, 2, 3, 4, 5, 6, 7, 8, 9, (pause) ten!" He places the club on the right shoulder of the 10th man, Acilius, who shudders with fear: The first of the three who brutally flagellated Yeshua. The Tribune continues counting off again. "1, 2, 3, 4, 5, 6, 7, 8, 9, (pause) ten!" He places the club on the right shoulder of the 10th man, Tarraco quakes.

Second of the three who brutally flagellated Yeshua pleads for reason, "We were overpowered by some unknown force."

The Tribune ignores him. "1, 2, 3, 4, 5, 6, 7, 8, 9, (pause) ten!"

Defiant, the thirtieth soldier, Creticus, shrugs the club off his right shoulder: The third of the three who brutally flagellated Yeshua. The Tribune has implemented the method of decimation whereby every tenth man is sentenced to death. The others will be spared. The Tribune points to the three. "You, you and you, step forward."

"The rest of you will camp outside the city for seven days and be given only barley."

The Tribune signals a soldier in the periphery to come forward with the heavy wooden clubs to distribute them to the other twenty-seven men. Centurion Lefus supervises, so the clubs are given out to all twenty-seven men. He directs them into two lines to form a corridor of men. The Tribune pushes the third defiant soldier, Creticus, ahead of the other two, Acilius and Tarraco, into the corridor. Lefus strikes his fist against the back of the first man in the line-up to commence the beating. Slowly the thumps begin to sound as the clubs fall on the condemned.

The Tribune pushes the two cowardly soldiers, Acilius and Tarraco, into the corridor toward the half-hearted beatings. The Tribune looks to Lefus and shakes his head to one side and another to show his disapproval. The combined force of the executioners will need encouragement. These men are faced with the unpleasant task of killing the men they have fought and worked with for years. Lefus grabs a club and begins an assault upon the backs of the twenty-seven men to motivate them. He cracks the shoulder of one man who flinches and collapses. The others see this result and increase their aggression against the three in the corridor.

Joseph of Arimathea turns away from the brutal action.

The clubs fall against the three, but some of the twenty-seven soldiers, attempt to avoid delivery of the beatings. Lefus, sees their reluctance, strikes them ever harder until they submit to carry out the punishment.

Slowly the renewed sound of the dull thump as club hits the target. Two sentenced soldiers stumble forward to catch up to the third soldier who stumbles. Former halfhearted swings have become forceful and savage. Cracks and cries of pain intensify with the breaking of human bones, loud screams, louder cries, groans, and shrieks permeate the blackness. Centurion Lefus steps aside to watch sadistically. Death for these three men is near at hand.

The Tribune walks to Joseph of Arimathea.

"You are free to go."

OUTSIDE JERUSALEM

An encampment of twenty-seven Roman soldiers sits around beyond the city walls: The campfire crackles. Centurion Lefus, the overseer, stands apart. Centurion Antonius rides a horse, approaches Lefus and dismounts. There is little these men have in common with one another. "They get their barley ration in the morning" Lefus says in a hurry to get away. Antonius tethers his horse.

The campfire embers glow, soldiers sleep, Antonius stands next to his horse and strokes the mane to calm them both. Time passes until an unidentifiable cloaked figure appears in the brush and stealthily approaches. Antonius' horse moves uneasily. Antonius, alert, takes a bearing on the cloaked figure who moves closer. He draws his sword. The cloaked figure proceeds directly.

He raises his sword. In Antonius' full view, she lowers her hood. Antonius sheaths his sword as Claudia enters his private space.

"What are you doing here?"

Claudia says quietly, intimately and intently, "We must find the Rabbi."

"The Rabbi was a Galilean and his followers were Galilean."

The horse pounds his hooves into the ground.

"We must go to Galilee."

"Claudia, how can I possibly go anywhere undetected with the wife of the Prefect?"

"My husband is different since the crucifixion of Yeshua."

The horse moves away sideways.

"I noticed."

"Then you must help me persuade my husband to go to Galilee."

He throws his arms up in the air.

"Then I will go alone." She turns on her heels and walks away determined.

The horse stomps his four hooves into the ground. Then sixteen hooves pound the dusty road.

In the distance, a small detachment of Roman Infantrymen led by four horses and their riders; Pontius, Claudia, Antonius and Mus, exit the city of Jerusalem.

ROME

Tiberius Caesar with Gaius Caligula, stand before a seated gallery of men, some seventy senators in session. Gaius with eccentricities and excesses, his desires, always wants to be center stage, his constant demands for recognition, a dangerous ego, he flirts with his audience to distract them. Gaius has the air of a malcontent. Caesar has made one of his very rare and short appearances. He prefers to rule remotely from Capreae.

"My nephew Gaius will one day be joint heir with Gemellus." Tiberius motions for Gaius to sit down and sit still. Ignoring Tiberius, instead of sitting nearby, he walks foppishly to the first row in the gallery and sits. His uncle makes allowances for young Caligula.

"My domicile, Capreae ..." As Tiberius continues, senators Aquila, a man about thirty-five, and scar-faced Vinicianus, huddle together on the top of the gallery. To one side, Vinicianus says quietly, "I would not want to be Gemellus." They instinctively know this puts Gemellus in jeopardy for his life. Senator Aquila shakes his head, a negative form of disbelief yet agreement with Vinicianus.

"Little Boots; big blunder." Aquila concedes, "Tiberius's heirs are not likely to work together." The two senators know Gaius well. Traits so well known to Vinicianus and Aquila, the two senators wonder why Tiberius cannot detect the warped personality of this boy.

JUDEA

After several weeks, his patience spent, Pontius focuses his line-of-sight. On the Mount of Olives in Judea some five hundred exuberant and joyful people, including eleven men, the Disciples of Yeshua, descend the mountain. Led by Pontius, accompanied by Mus, Claudia and Antonius, on horseback, they halt with apprehension, exchange questioning looks, to observe the crowd. They see an intimidating number compared to the small group of Romans. Pontius, Mus and Antonius position themselves to meet them head-on. Claudia places her horse behind the three of them.

"Antonius, bring one of those men to me."

Antonius rides ahead and out of earshot and speaks to them. After a short exchange, Antonius returns with a man from the group, who is of average height, with dark curly hair.

Andrew, a young man, walks with Antonius, who rides, up to the three horsemen. Pontius has the first word.

"What are you celebrating?"

"Yeshua has ascended."

"Ascended?"

"Yeshua of Nazareth, who was crucified, dead and buried."

The happy mob flows around Pontius who looks awkwardly at Antonius. "His dead body is here on this mountain?"

"Our Master has risen and is alive again."

More of the smiles from the other ten disciples include Yachanan and Kefa. The core group of Hebrews gathers, disciples of Yeshua. While the greater crowd flows out and around the Romans. The masses have an appearance of hysterical happiness. Their smiles become disconcerting to Pontius. "Are you drunk?" He asks in all seriousness. They all laugh. The happy mob keeps moving.

"Our Master spent forty days with us." Andrew says. He expressly directs his statement to Pontius. Antonius studies the man. Pontius looks around the mob. Claudia, listens, and moves her horse forward.

"Take me to this man you call Master, so I might identify him."

"He has ascended."

"Ascended, where?"

Andrew looks up to the sky. Pontius turns to Antonius.

"Have the men search this mob for 'their Master'."

The few troops they have with them walk calmly unimpeded toward the mountain. The Prefect asks Andrew, "Describe this man you speak of." The mob happily makes way for the Romans as Pontius remains focused on Andrew.

"His raiment is like silver ..."

"No, no, no, no, what does he looks like?"

Antonius and Mus stand-by, listen and protect Claudia and Pontius.

"You know what he looks like," Andrew says to disarm the Prefect.

Impulsively, Claudia interjects, "The Rabbi."

Andrew looks at Claudia, points at her and nods agreement.

Not making progress, Pontius tries yet again, "The Rabbi is dead but this other man, the ascended one you speak of looks like him?"

"His brilliant eyes read into the 'hearts and minds' of all men."

Pontius pulls on the reins of his horse.

"Yes, yes, yes, a magician who plays tricks. Nonsense."

"Yeshua, the man you scourged and crucified," Andrew adds without prejudice.

Pontius glares at Andrew.

With hope and promise, Andrew begins, "He told us all about you!"

Pontius has heard enough.

"Antonius! Call the men. We waste our time here."

Antonius makes sweeping arm movements as the Roman troops re-group. The other eleven men and the five hundred happily continue on their way. Led on horseback by Pontius, followed by Mus, Claudia and Antonius, the Roman troops march solemnly back to the city.

16

AQUEDUCT

THE ANTONIA FORTRESS

Pontius sits behind a large table to study the various large parchments rolled out in front of him. Business for the Prefect includes his determination to build two aqueducts to bring water into the city of Jerusalem. He looks down at the plans. Engineering, a pursuit with practical benefits, unlike looking for the mysterious disappearance of a dead body; an experience he prefers to forget: Although it is something that nags at his conscience, as much as he attempts to ignore it.

Caiaphas is one key to the success of the aqueduct. To gain the necessary funds for the building he knows he will have to exert pressure on the Chief Priest. Pontius also knows he will never be able to gain his respect, or the results he wishes for, in a cooperative manner. So, he must enter the fray with a certain amount of abandon. Pontius cannot resist being unpolitic sometimes. By virtue of the Chief Priest's position, he is forced by circumstances to engage in conversation with him. Antonius stands alongside Caiaphas as if to protect the Prefect. He keeps his head down in the parchments.

"Our search for the stolen body of your Rabbi *King* has not produced results." For effect he looks up knowing he touches the pride of this man Caiaphas by purposefully using the word "King." It brings forth the response Pontius expects which is not the best way to begin negotiations, but he succeeds to irritate and intimidate Caiaphas. Centurion Antonius, as always, a quiet interested observer.

"He was not our *king*." Caiaphas objects, offended at the title given to the man he criminalized.

Now intent to unnerve the Chief Priest, he delivers with cheek and whimsy. "Possessed of drink and hysterics, a mob said your Yeshua, your prince, your savior, He is alive again," The jest plays with the facts as he knows them. The Prefect's attempt at frivolity to unravel his own thoughts, perhaps tests himself. Pontius goads the Chief Priest, with smiles, hardly the very best means by which to obtain an advantage over Caiaphas for the benefit of the aqueduct. Caiaphas stands erect, considers his response while Pontius pushes a point of importance. Perhaps deep down the Prefect instinctively knows that something very significant for the Yehudim people has taken place. The mere suggestion that Yeshua may be alive gives Pontius some amusement and satisfaction. Perhaps he wants to believe it.

When Pontius allows himself to reflect upon the trial of Yeshua. He recalls it has touched him in various ways; a conviction of the man who was definitely innocent. And there was a series of natural events that took place during the execution that cannot be fully explained; the fact Yeshua died more quickly than is usual in these cases when one is nailed to wood, a normally very slow torturous death; the earthquakes; the darkening of the sun and sky; the shining stars; the red moon; the opening of tombs; the walking dead; the damage to the temple; the sheer force needed to break the iron seal of the tomb door; the soldiers who "fell down like dead men" and simultaneously the body of Yeshua disappears. Pontius confirms his respect for two men that Caiaphas believes have been brain-washed.

He fails to make Caiaphas respond to his statement that Yeshua is alive again, he presses forth with some newly gained knowledge of their history. "Nicodemus and Joseph say the events confirm what was spoken of by Isaiah, your prophet."

"You know nothing!"

"Yeshua was killed by you. Yeshua replaced the bleating lambs you sacrifice for your sins, your rebellions against your YeHoVaH." Pontius stands up, moves around the desk. Caiaphas, speechless, captured in the vacuum Pontius fills. "Yeshua was silent during the trial. I *never* understood why he would *not* defend himself. Isaiah predicted he would remain *'dumb'* so now it begins to make sense. Yeshua's death was his plan for you, preordained by your YeHoVaH."

The Chief Priest cannot contain his building aggression and the repugnance for such suggestions any longer. "*Our* Messiah will come as a warrior! You know nothing." Pontius has listened to commentary, reevaluated his understanding and puzzlement of the Trial to further open his mind as no means a solution yet but a slow change that continues in him. A mystery the Prefect attempts to unravel.

Pontius paces. He pauses, looks intently at Caiaphas. Still unaware of why he has been drawn into this meeting with Pontius. He has Caiaphas balanced on one foot by shaking his rigid doctrine. The Prefect cannot resist the opportunity to group The Chief Priest in with all the murderers, one in particular. He wants Caiaphas in a defensive position. He wants to humiliate him. He wants him to be guilty by association.

"'Warrior' huh. You say so, and so does your friend Barabbas!"

Pontius looks intently at him again and then turns his attention back to the parchments and the model of the aqueduct. The association with Barabbas grips his tongue and binds Caiaphas. For once perhaps Pontius has dominance over Caiaphas. The Prefect swings into the real topic of the day and directs his stare at the work of the draftsmen.

"Jerusalem needs water. The cost to build an aqueduct exceeds all our Roman collections." Without any attempt at tact, he makes his demands plain. "Your people will pay for this." Pontius looks up for the challenge.

"The people cannot be taxed anymore."

"Money changes hands in the temple." Pontius adds avariciously, "Where is that money kept?"

Trying to gain back his strength with resistance to the Prefect's demands he objects, "That money is sanctified."

Pontius knows this claim will be difficult to overcome when a proprietary interest is invested in the name of YeHoVaH, a God the Roman Prefect has nearly disregarded. So, he baits the arrogant Chief Priest. "What? Sanctified?"

"It belongs to YeHoVaH."

Pontius moves in and raises his hands in acceptance. "Very well: YeHoVaH will pay to build this aqueduct."

Caiaphas, haughty and prideful, abruptly walks out. Antonius swings around to see him leave. Pontius says to his wife's cousin, perceptively thinking through Antonius's likely discomfort, "You should have kept your money. Don't worry; this is a job for your colleague."

THE TEMPLE

Pontius orders Lefus to use the dark hours for surprise. At night some distance from the Temple a cohort of Roman soldiers march with oxen and an empty cart. Inside the perimeter wall, an enclosure, "The Court of the Women", deserted except for the four Temple Guards who stand in the right-hand-corner. One guard being Malchus, whose ear was cut off by Peter and miraculously replaced by Yeshua.

Malchus turns his head using his restored ear to listen: The ominous sound of marching footsteps. A wave of Roman Soldiers flows through the perimeter wall, expand into the courtyard, many hold burning torches. The four Temple Guards brace themselves, overwhelmingly outnumbered.

Centurion Lefus is the first to make demands, "Open that door!" He points to the reinforced door behind which all the funds are locked. Given by the people for the temple or taken from the poor people? One wonders what amount may have been contributed by the money changers.

"By whose authority?" asks Malchus.

"By order, of Pontius Pilate, the Prefect of Judea and Samaria."

"The Treasury cannot be entered without ..."

"Drop your weapons." Lefus motions his men forward swiftly.

The Roman Soldiers quickly rush to seize three of the Temple Guards.

"Grab him!" Simultaneously four soldiers swiftly spill Malchus onto his back pulling each limb so he cannot move. Lefus unsheathes his sword, places the tip of it under Malchus' tunic.

"Pull him up slowly." The Roman Soldiers raise him by the arms so the pressure of the blade of his sword on his chest cuts the fabric of his tunic.

Struck with fear Malchus pleads, "I will open the door."

They stand him up and pull him to the door and shove him against it. Lefus holds his sword against Malchus who takes a key, unlocks the door and opens it. Lefus gestures and the soldiers hold burning torches, enter all four of the buildings at each corner of the courtyard.

Six soldiers exit the treasury. They struggle with a large, heavy chest. "Open it!" Inside the chest is full of coins. Lefus waves his arms, signals the soldiers to follow him, and enters the treasury. Soldiers exit the vault carrying the twelve heavy chests through the courtyard toward the carts. The soldiers stack the cart with the chests; the oxen wait obediently. The Temple Guards can do nothing but stand and watch. Plunder has been easy. Caiaphas will be less wealthy.

THE POOLS OF SOLOMON

Construction of the aqueduct has commenced. Pontius and the Ingeniare, both on horseback, plus a small contingent of Roman Soldiers, including Mus, inspect one of the three pools of Solomon. As the horses and riders stroll along, they are unaware of approaching danger.

Bandits emerge, unseen by Pontius; The Sicarii, climb the banks of the pool, five of them, cloaked, carry daggers. Undetected, they sneak along the bank.

In the distance, a workforce of scores of men, dig into the dry ground sending up a cloud of dust to obscure their activity. Suddenly, bandits jump on top of the Roman detail like violent baboons!

With little time for the Romans to draw their swords, hand-to-hand combat ensues. Pontius, dragged down off his horse, lands on his feet, struggles to hold back the dagger being thrust near his face by the biggest bandit in the group! The struggle, hand holds, the bandit's plunging dagger now threatens Pontius's abdomen. Like a dance, the rabid bandit wrestles to put the Prefect off-balance.

The Ingeniare, Antonius and Lefus, swords drawn, swing violently at their assailants to keep them out of dagger-range, four of them counter attack.

Pontius falls to the ground, overpowered by the bigger man.

Mus digs his heels into the flanks of his horse, gallops into their midst, and forces the animal to rear-up over Pontius and the bandit. The flailing front hooves tower above him. The bandit gives Pontius one final thrust with the dagger, he resists, and the bandit falls over to one side, releases himself, and runs away.

The other four bandits see his escape, and follow in haste as Antonius and Lefus give chase. Mus retrieves the horses. The Centurions return empty-handed. Pontius brushes the dust off his tunic.

THE ANTONIA FORTRESS

Caiaphas stands defiant and impatient in an anti-room of the Antonia Fortress. "Return it all! At once!"

Outside the fortress the crowd can be heard chanting, "The governor is a thief."

Pontius calmly walks to a table upon which rests many bowls of fresh fruit. He takes a large orange and hands it to Caiaphas, who refuses to accept it.

"Tiberius Caesar will not be pleased with you!"

Pontius tears open the orange to relish the juice and quietly says; "You know all elected officers are appointed by Rome. Most prefects serve a few years." He shouts, "I have been here for eight years!"

Far from intimidated, Caiaphas believes he can dislodge the position Pontius thinks is consolidated. In a fury he retaliates, "Tiberius Caesar will remove you unless you return our treasury!"

Pontius with disdain in his voice, "What do you use to think with?" He holds up the eaten orange squeezed in his fist.

Then blasts him with, "Is it like this pulp? When all the goodness has gone out of it?" Pontius turns and begins to leave the room. "Lefus, escort him out!"

Stopping, he calls after him in a fury. "I try to help your people. All I get from you is resistance; rumors of revolt, an attempt on my life! Because of this!?" He takes a pitcher of water, in fine pottery, and throws it across the room; it shatters against the wall.

The crowds outside the Antonia Fortress continue to shout: "The Governor is a thief!" "The Governor is a thief!" Pontius stands still listening, quietly seething.

Later, Roman Soldiers exit the fortress and filter into the crowd, cloaked in garments which conceal their uniforms; the same fabrics as those worn by the mob. Under their cloaks, every disguised soldier ominously carries a dagger. Caiaphas makes his way through the mob to spread unrest to denounce the Prefect as a thief. The disguised soldiers mingle throughout like the contents of a sieve are lightly sprinkled into the dense ground.

On top of the fortress wall Pontius, flanked by Antonius and Lefus, looks out across the crowds who have grown to some ten thousand strong! One member of the masses below notices Pontius has come out on the wall. He shouts upwards to him; "No aqueduct! Return the treasury!"

Another adds, "Thief!"

Pontius looks to both of his Centurions and shakes his head in disbelief. He raises his hands in the air and waits for the bedlam to calm down; it does not. Hands remain held high, he mutters to his Centurions, "They refuse to listen to reason." He lowers his hands, exasperated. The Tribune enters to join them on top of the wall.

"The men are in place," the Tribune informs Pontius. During the trial of Yeshua, when Pontius became terrified of Yeshua and the growing possibility the pilgrims would revolt, he sent an urgent message to Vitellius, the Legate of Syria, a large province to the north. The Tribune has travelled with a legion, as requested by Pontius. The legion was too late to put down a possible insurrection then, but they were retained. Now it appears their good use has been found. As a group of fighting men, they are ready to release the building of tensions, the boredoms of waiting for battle. Pontius, hesitates, and looks into the crowd. He puts his hands out to Antonius and Lefus, takes their bludgeons, and holds them high for all to see. Clenching his jaw with quiet anger he brings down the bludgeons to rest on the top of the wall.

At ground level a scuffle nearby, one man strikes another. Red blood drips from a head wound as the victim slumps to the ground. Those around the disguised soldier step back. His garment parts open to expose more weaponry. Further in the crowd, another victim falls in the dust.

Barabbas, now fully recovered from his time of imprisonment, the beatings and starvation enters at the rear periphery of the mob.

At random, the crowd opens around a fallen victim. Then the mass heaves and attempts to disperse, and run away, only to be attacked in the rear by the disguised soldiers.

Caiaphas panics, trying to leave in the turmoil.

The crowd jostles to find an escape for itself, like ebb and flow tide, the waves get bigger. Barabbas pushes in against the flow.

A wounded civilian staggers and runs off. Many trips and fall defenseless to the ground, trampled and then slain. Brutally bludgeoned without mercy or concern for their frailty of age, young and old, male or female, they fall easy prey.

On top of the wall, distant, Pontius and Antonius, wave frantically, unseen, try to get the attention of the troops, to cease and desist, without result. Pontius raises the bludgeons.

Caiaphas flees, runs smack into Barabbas, who hesitates. Trapped and jostled by the mob, two disguised Roman Soldiers recognize fine clothes: They recognize Caiaphas as Barabbas backs away defensively. The younger, fit Barabbas runs into the throng. The blood spills as the soldiers substitute bludgeons for swords, like packs of wolves, wildly keep tearing into the flock, which stampede in retreat.

Barabbas succeeds and forces his way through but only to impale himself on the dagger of a disguised Roman who grins mercilessly at his kill. Barabbas slumps to the ground. Caiaphas escapes.

Pontius and Antonius raise their bludgeons and cross them as a signal to halt the attack. The flailing soldiers continue their attack. Lefus and the Tribune exchange looks of complacence. Pontius angrily drops the bludgeons and raises two swords and waves them frantically in an attempt to save lives. None of the soldiers look back, they merely push forward slaying all that fail to get away.

Pontius shouts at the Tribune "Go down there and stop them!" The Tribune exits. Pontius shows a feeling of concern akin with Antonius, unlike the Tribune and Lefus. Could this be maturity or a slow change within him?

The Tribune walks unimpeded. The Roman Soldiers have scared the mod. In haste to escape, the scattering crowd knocked down the feeble. The Tribune stops the bloodshed. The Soldiers, ordered back into the barracks, still have much fight left in them. The Tribune allows the injured to crawl away.

The earth exposed reveals the bloody dead who litter the dusty ground.

17
MASSACRE

THE ANTONIA FORTRESS

Two Roman guards struggle to hold up a Samaritan man in torn clothes. He has bruises, a swollen eye, and dried blood all over him. He is barely conscious. Pontius sits at his desk in the judgement hall of the fortress. Pontius has listened while the interrogators expose the plot to overthrow Roman rule in Samaria.

Antonius and Lefus turn to see the Tribune enter with Caiaphas. "Prefect, Caiaphas begs your indulgence."

Pontius closes his eyes, incredulous, and shakes his head. Stunned that the Tribune would interrupt the Prefect he quietly says. "No, I know why he is here."

Caiaphas says, "Prefect! You have stolen from our Temple and butchered my people. They were unarmed innocents."

Claudia avoids being noticed as she enters and stays within earshot, but hidden.

Caiaphas sees the Samaritan sprawled on the floor. He points at the man.

"Recognize a Samaritan?" Pontius says sarcastically because he knows the Samaritans hate the Yehudim.

"Oh." Caiaphas studies the victim but stays on point. "Your brutality will come to the attention of Tiberius."

The Tribune also brings Nicodemus into the party. Flabbergasted, Pontius asks, "What? What in the name of Mercury, Jupiter, and Neptune, or YeHoVaH, and now you, a follower of Yeshua, what are you here for?" Pontius mixes all the doctrines to get their reaction. When in fact his subconscious provokes more serious thoughts; the knowledge of YeHoVaH and Yeshua as informed by Nicodemus has lodged in his consciousness and he is unable to dislodge it.

Nicodemus looks at Caiaphas then Pontius. "The Samaritans plan to raise an army to take Mount Gerizim."

Caiaphas, distracted by the interruption, forgets his main import to complain about the people's resistance to the theft of treasury coins, the subsequent Roman ambush and viscous killing of unarmed Yehudim. At a tangent he claims, "The Samaritans have violated our sacred laws!"

"Changes in *your* own laws, to suit *your*selves?" Amused, Pontius sits down to gloat.

Nicodemus adds, "Their leader claims he is the new messiah."

"Tell me something I do not know," Pontius states in a remarkably calm manner as if a new man within him tolerates the circus that unfolds around him. Where is his disdain for Caiaphas?

"Because those heathen Samaritans disobeyed His law, our God YeHoVaH sent in lions to kill them," says Caiaphas who seems completely distracted from the reason he came to see the Prefect. His hate for the Samaritans exceeds and takes precedence above the love for his own people.

Claudia listens intently.

"You are an unruly savage lion," the Chief Priest accuses The Prefect, who seems to transfer all his own guilt in one fell swoop. Caiaphas keeps the blame focused on Pontius. Superficially amused at the ridiculous flattery and comparison with lion, he wonders when Caiaphas will recognize the seriousness of the new overall situation.

"You are fortunate your God YeHoVaH did not set the lions upon you," adds Pontius who knows he has lost control of the meeting and seems to enjoy it for amusement.

"Neither Mount Gerizim, nor our temple, is necessary to worship YeHoVaH." Nicodemus, one of the few prepared to stand up to the Chief Priest, continues, "Yeshua resides within us, if we are born again." (adapted John 3:1-8)

"Nicodemus!" Caiaphas warns his brain-washed colleague, "You are in danger of committing blasphemy."

"Yeshua is the living temple." Nicodemus boldly adds, "That damaged building is an accessory and the living Temple of Yeshua is within us. If you believe in Him." Caiaphas is aghast at such teachings that undermine his power, his politics and his income.

Pontius remembers why The Chief Priest's presence protests the action his men took to ambush the crowd. He cuts in with a smile, "So you will *not* require the temple funds," because the Prefect has been justified by Nicodemus.

"Don't listen to Nicodemus! His mind has been vacated!"

This diagnosis falls lightly on the ears of Pontius, the man whose conscience has been weighed down heavily with reflections on the trial of Yeshua. No doubt he feels slightly vindicated and less guilty for being the executioner.

"Vacated? All of it?" asks Pontius with his whimsy and also a sense of his growing knowledge.

"He is under the spell of that man Yeshua, the man *you* crucified!" Caiaphas reminds him so there should be no doubt where the blame lies.

Pontius changes tone, to recall the words of Yeshua, pointing unequivocally and directly at Caiaphas, "He said, 'your sin is greater than mine.'" Shaken but undeterred Caiaphas focusses to recalculate the sins on the Samaritans.

Nicodemus moves around, points at the fallen man, "His kind is the present threat, a false Messiah; we have been warned." Pontius nudges the fallen man who groans.

"They have perverted our laws and our God would have them slain, by you Prefect!" Caiaphas says to the Prefect who tires of being told what to do. "You are justified by God," an amazingly clever trick to play on a Roman who believes nothing; the Chief Priest plays his cunning game bidding the Prefect to do his work for them again.

Pontius, now more serious, listens. "So, we will settle the disputes between you and your enemies?" Pontius wonders when will the Chief Priest return to the matter of finance for the aqueduct, the use of the temple treasury?

"If you don't, they will unseat the rule of Rome here in Samaria and Judea." Caiaphas threatens. Pontius can only seethe as he comes under this constant intimidation.

Nicodemus looks pointedly at Caiaphas and back at Pontius. "The Samaritans are a danger to our peace, but they have few weapons to match the Romans. Nicodemus turns around again on Caiaphas, deriding him. "You were incredulously wrong. Yeshua was innocent. This Oseos ..."

"Enough! Enough!" Pontius, nerves touched again by the mention of the innocent Yeshua, stands up and moves between them. Their combined manipulation and control anger the Prefect. He dropped his public guard, but now re-erects it.

Annoyed, he turns to Antonius. "Antonius, the Samaritans appear to be just as crazy as your Yehudim friends!" In a serious mood now, slowly, quietly comes to the boil, Pontius paces the floor, back and forth. "Again ..." Pontius turns threateningly to face Caiaphas. "I am again to wield the sword for you and your God YeHoVaH?"

Claudia remains in the shadows motionless transfixed by the tension.

Seriously he contemplates his actions, Pontius's eyes dance between Antonius and Lefus and the Tribune then swings around at the two Yehudim. "Moses! Your prophet. Delivered your people from slavery." Pontius has their silent attention which he uses. "A new reincarnated Moses will find the sacred vessels hidden by the former prophet Moses, on Mount Gerizim. Or left by Oseos, and when found, they identify the new Samaritan messiah?" He pauses to consider the circumstances and then angry, he blurts out, "All of this is craziness beyond reason!"

Antonius picks up the essence of the plan, nods agreement at Pontius. Without missing the inference in Antonius' demeanor, Pontius comprehends the threat of another uprising.

"Ah ha. Another Messiah." Pontius stands and walks around the fallen man.

Lefus, ever ready for a fight, uses what influence he has, "This new Messiah will lead the Samaritans to freedom."

"Huh!" Pontius motions to the two guards to drag the fallen man away. "Antonius, these Samaritans appear to be *crazier* than your Yehudim friends!"

In a more serious mood, Pontius paces the floor, back and forth. Samaritan zeal will substitute for the lack of Samaritan armaments. Religious fervor, Pontius knows from experience, can be more powerful than the sword. While he contemplates his actions, his eyes dance between Antonius and Lefus and the Tribune. He looks directly at Nicodemus and Caiaphas, "I am left again, with no other choice." His tone of defeat belies his reluctance for more bloodshed.

TIRATHABA

The Samaritans with boldness and excitement rally in the streets telling their fellow villagers to arm themselves for victory. They grow in numbers collecting crude weapons of clubs and knives. They incite themselves, into religious fever, a near frenzied riot of rebellion. They lack the armaments of a slower professional, a well-equipped military order and rush to the gate.

MOUNT GERIZIM

The column of Romans, cavalry and infantry, over a legion strong, kick up the dust along the trail to the mountain. Reaching the plain at the base of Mount Gerizim they form a wedge, equidistant, between the village of Tirathaba and the foot of the mountain. The wedge points toward the village.

Pontius, Antonius and Lefus, on horseback, stand on a rise overlooking the plain, the troops and the land below, toward Tirathaba. A cohort stands-by to protect the Prefect. Strategy has been worked out. Pontius believes a show of force will overwhelm the Samaritans and that intimidation will do the battle for them.

Samaritans swarm out of the village in an unruly riot and widen their forward progress as they head for the base of the mountain. One of them rushes ahead, an obvious leader, a mad man. The Roman troops block the road. The Samaritans run to face Roman shields and javelins that create an impenetrable barrier. The Samaritans near the Roman troops falter and stop. The Samaritan leader rushes forward alone, flailing his club, possessed of insanity as if he could intimidate a Roman army. He calls upon his Samaritans to advance and they naturally spill and therefore split down the angled sides of the wedge.

The Roman troops following hand-orders from the Tribune push out to the sides from the middle.

With shields in a defensive straight line, they open up a corridor to let the mad man through, unscathed, with some followers. In the midst of the Roman army, he screams and shouts the crazed ranting of a false victory as he runs through the middle, "God has shown us the way." The Romans have succeeded in dividing the Samaritans into three sections, one on each flank and the middle section led by the total maniacal, hand-waving, mad man. This Samaritan moves forward into the middle of the Roman corridor. He beckons to encourage them, "God is with us."

The Tribune on horseback descends the rise to the battlefield followed by cavalry. Then eagerly, the Tribune stops, signals by moving his arms in and out latitudinal: The shielded Roman corridor further widens. The Samaritans on either flank get pushed further apart. The Samaritans in the middle march forward into the widening Roman corridor. The mad man reaches the far side of the Roman formation and declares victory, jumping hysterically.

Another band of Samaritans exits the village and makes haste to catch-up with the first contingent.

The middle section of Roman troops closes to surround the Samaritans in the corridor. The Romans take prisoners, beat them to the ground and then tie them with vines. This apparent act of mercy has been sanctioned by a generous Pontius. The Tribune directs commands at his troops. As resistance mounts, however, those Samaritans who put up a fight are slain. In this Roman attempt to take prisoners, Samaritans begin to escape, slip free, run for freedom. The Romans find it easier to cut down an escapee than to tie him up.

From the rise Pontius can see the escalation of mayhem as the Roman formation becomes less defined. Pontius turns to Centurion Lefus. "Command the Tribune. Push them into retreat back to their village." Lefus signals the Cohort and makes haste. They gallop. Infantrymen follow down the slope.

The second Samaritan contingent, now close enough to see the bloody mayhem, stop and look on in terror.

The Tribune and his cavalry join in the massacre. Some Samaritans with fast legs carry no protective uniforms or equipment unlike the Romans. They are able to outrun the soldiers and escape to hide in bushes, ravines, and up the mountain.

The second contingent of Samaritans fixated for moments, turns and runs back toward the village. Lefus and the cohort chase the second retreating contingent of Samaritans into the village.

From the rise Pontius fumes at Antonius! "Divert Lefus and the Tribune to circle them all! Push them all back to the village!" Antonius gallops down the slope with two cavalrymen.

Lefus and the Tribune chase the second wave of Samaritans as they near Tirathaba. Antonius catches up to direct Lefus and the Tribune to turn back, to round up the first wave but they ignore him.

"Turn back that's an order. You have them on the run. Round-up those." He points to the Samaritans who are tangled in engagement. "Push them back to the village."

Lefus looks at Antonius with contempt and chases the retreating Samaritans into the village. He cuts down all, without regard; old men, young men, punching, pummeling and pushing aside women and children alike, without mercy.

Antonius and the two cavalrymen turn to the first wave of Samaritans near the base of the mountain. Encircled by the Roman troops, those without legs quick enough to run away are slain without hesitation. The mad man has fallen. Antonius, late to prevent the total annihilation of the Samaritans, looks up to the top of the hill.

Pontius surveys this battlefield with utter dismay, the carnage not intended. Repeatedly, in Jerusalem, he has been unable to control the collateral damage. He orders his commanders back to the hilltop. He has private regrets. Also, he has to maintain a public role. He has prevented an uprising with brutal military might. The foolhardiness of the losers, their blind faith in nothing but myth, has cost them depletion in population far in excess of any good reason. Pontius must accept this as the cost of his success, but he cannot rest easy.

He awaits the withdrawal of his men. They reform to march and leave the battle ground strewn with bodies. As his commanders reassemble, he lectures them. "Know when to attack and when to withdraw. This victory was won from the start. Our overwhelming strength and superiority sufficient to ensure success, measured to favor the result. To get them to give up and run: They ran. This butchery was utterly not necessary."

CAESAREA MARITTIMA

Several days later word has travelled over the region. The massacre of the Samaritans has pleased the Hebrew subjects. Music and Hebrew dancers perform for Pontius. His residence, in Herod's palace at Caesarea, lifts the sprits in a celebratory festive mood for many except Pontius. Roman officers of the legion and their wives, toast one another. Pontius and Claudia sit at the head table, and enjoy the entertainment, on the surface.

In the past such military action would be of no consequence; he just does his job. Claudia recognizes her husband's nature appears to soften. Sumptuous freshly made foods, wine; a sufficient amount to make their eyes sparkle at one another but Claudia knows her husband internalizes an illness of ease and a regret unlike she has seen in him ever before. They try to put the memory of this massacre behind them but it is not possible.

A soldier approaches Centurion Lefus, who whispers in his ear. Lefus rises and leaves; Pontius notices Lefus leave. The merriment continues. Lefus returns, approaches Pontius, bends to his ear and Pontius gestures approval. Lefus signals.

In walks Marcellus, a young visiting Roman. Well-groomed, he approaches Pontius directly, who immediately motions him to sit down with them. "Forgive me for interrupting your evening." Marcellus says with an undertone of regret.

"Huh. Our celebrations. Sit Marcellus." Shira brings Marcellus a goblet and fills it from a leather wine skin decanter. Awkwardly, Marcellus nods his acceptance. He really does not want this mission which he has been given by his superior but he has to follow orders.

Lefus follows Shira to another room while Pontius has his focus elsewhere.

"What does my friend Lucius Vitellius, the esteemed Legate of Syria, have for me? A promotion? Ha Ha!"

"We should talk after the celebrations."

"Hum. When one quashes a rebellion, three of them in fact, one could be called to do so, again and again, over a wider area!?"

Marcellus shifts in his seat. "That may be so." Pontius studies him less happily.

Claudia glares at Marcellus intently as she intuitively picks up the sense of unease about him. Pontius doesn't like his demeanor. As a reflex, he stands. Claudia does the same. They walk out to leave Marcellus ponder their displeasure.

They hear Shira's voice, "No! Lefus, if you touch me again, I shall scream." Claudia and Pontius enter the kitchen, but Shira is out of sight. They hear muffled noises come from the pantry. As they enter, Lefus has Shira pinned against the wall and his hand now covers her mouth. Pontius takes a wooden utensil off the shelf and rams it into his kidney. Lefus groans and releases Shira as he slumps to the ground. Claudia takes Shira by the hand to extricate her. She steps over the wounded Lefus. Pontius takes a long hard silent disapproving look at Lefus and leaves.

The next morning Pontius looks out over the ocean. Claudia says, "You suspect Marcellus."

"I do." Pontius knows good news is rarely withheld. Bad news is timed. "He is here to demote me."

Marcellus enters. He holds a small scroll. A deflected greeting, Marcellus looks out and notices, "The sea is calm this morning."

"Huh. How is Lucius Vitellius?" Pontius wants to get to business.

"He is well."

"Good. Then no plague or uprising has befallen him."

Claudia hands Marcellus a goblet.

"The legate of Syria has the country under his control." Marcellus implies this is not so in Judea and Samaria.

Pontius walks to the table and sits down and with well-chosen words and formal precision, "The seriousness of your demeanor gives portent to your ominous message Marcellus."

Marcellus looks at Claudia. Pontius changes tone, becomes increasingly impatient with him, uses the vernacular, "Why don't you spit it out man!?"

"Perhaps we should speak in private."

"Why? That I should not report to my wife, that which you have come here to tell me?"

Claudia sits down.

"Very well" Marcellus takes a drink. "Immediately after your attack and massacre of the Samaritans at Mount Gerizim a delegation presented charges of murder to Vitellius, charges against you."

Pontius replies with some venom, "Soldiers do not commit murder when they defend our empire."

"Let him finish" Claudia quickly interjects.

"They reported to Vitellius that upon your command your soldiers went into the Samaritan village of Tirathaba, and slaughtered their men, women and children."

Impatient with the charges against him, Pontius says "That is preposterous. The Samaritans raised an army against Rome. We were routing that army." He could not inform Marcellus his troops were over-excitable going on a killing spree against his wishes. Because that would be an admission that he lost control of his men.

"I am not here to pass judgement ..."

"I succeeded, put down this revolt swiftly, with no loss of life to our men."

"What would you have had my husband do?"

"It is not for me to say. However, no Roman casualties, commendable in itself, suggests to me the Samaritans were not in a position to resist."

He passes the small scroll to Pontius.

"Is this my husband's commendation or his condemnation?"

"I can see which way this is going!" as Pontius opens and studies the scroll.

"Vitellius requires that you return to Rome immediately. I will oversee Judea and Samaria until ..."

"Until the next prophet, the next Oseos, next Moses, the next Rabbi, next Messiah, next king, the next Yeshua opposes our occupation here?"

"Tiberius Caesar will hear your defense."

"And then Vitellius will be sorry he has listened to the defeated Samaritans instead of me, the victor, and the Hebrews who are enjoying this peace. Any hope of my own salvation has been dashed by this."

Pontius rolls the scroll back up and slaps it in his other hand. He looks disdainfully upon an uncomfortable Marcellus. Claudia walks out on Marcellus to signal her disgust and to regain her composure.

18

EMPEROR GOD

March 16th 37 AD

CAPREAE

On the island of Capreae inside Caesar's palace Tiberius lies prone on a large bed. He is aged, shriveled and weak. In attendance, an academic and an astrologer, hover over him. Tiberius knows his last breath is not too far distant. His preference to live a secluded life away from the big city and rule remotely has provided him with a sense of security. Assassins, the fear of every ruler in Rome, have not yet found their way to his island. The children he has abused have not threatened him because he has dispatched them over the cliff. Natural causes may take Tiberius's life away from him or someone may help him on his way. The present whereabouts of his nephew Gaius Caligula is unknown.

Tiberius delegated responsibilities of command through his ambitious pro-consul Sejanus. Tiberius hoped Sejanus would take the temporary responsibilities of state until his nephews are old enough to rule. Gaius Caligula's fine education, a credit to his uncle, if one includes debauchery, kidnapping and homicide as acceptable. Sejanus, however, falls from grace. Tiberius, in a weakened condition concedes his nephews forthcoming rule, "There is nothing we can do about it. Gaius and Gemellus, succeed me."

One of the Academics moves closer, no doubt to engage the dying Caesar to distract him from his fate, "Pontius Pilate killed thousands of innocent Yehudim and Samaritans." The recall of the Prefect of Judea and Samaria is known to Tiberius in a communication from Vitellius, the Legate of Syria. Pontius, in transit across the blue seas, has no news yet that his defender Tiberius decays rapidly.

A Physician enters the bedroom and leans over a table to mix a tonic. The astrologer adds more accusations, "Pilate misused the temple funds of Jerusalem; murdered those who objected."

"He crucified an innocent teacher who was loved by his people!" the academic says.

"I will give him a fair trial." Tiberius says weakly, "If I am still alive."

Tiberius holds onto his slim life with a political purpose, to return to rule and adjudicate. "We must hear what Pontius Pilate has achieved during his Prefecture before my nephew can pervert the course of justice."

Deliriousness like a swinging pendulum takes his mind from optimism to pessimism and back again. "Where is Gaius?" The academic and the astrologer look doubtfully at one another. The academic rearranges his pillows. The physician helps Tiberius take his tonic. Time and nature converge, inevitably.

ROME, THE PALACE OF GAIUS CALIGULA

Gaius Caligula looks at Pontius without a hint of threat. He recalls but does not acknowledge that the Prefect extricated him from the embarrassment of falling from his horse. Now some ten years after that foolish accident, Gaius at age twenty-four is still ugly. In addition, he is balding, tall, pale and lithe. Forever the exhibitionist and on this occasion has chosen the costume of the Greco-Roman god Apollo. No one knows why. Sober, his manners affected, exaggerated, patronizing, but not without a strange charm. His palace is beautiful and sumptuous. He sits regally in a theatrical way like a bad actor who expects his audience to love his performance anyway.

"My late uncle Tiberius trusted you with his Yehudim."

Pontius stands erect and looks ahead seriously.

In the background, two Praetorian Guards stand on either side of pillars at the entrance way. Caligula picks up a small harp and plucks it discordantly.

"Your talent is with horses." Pontius attempts to make light of the situation he is in and he will try to hide the contempt he has for Gaius. Caligula has not missed this slight put down but overlooks it. Pontius's suspicions include the possibility that Gaius has murdered both his Uncle Tiberius and cousin Gemellus. The Prefect knows his defense of his actions in the eastern lands would have been held more credulous by Tiberius. Gaius, he knows, will twist for the best of theater, any way he chooses.

"The Samaritans were looking for lost gold?" Gaius wishes to express his knowledge to impress the young lady, an obvious ally, who enters and sits down to watch the proceedings like a game.

"They recruited an army." Pontius looks around as another young woman with a senator enter. He is Vinicianus, memorable for the battle scar on his face.

"To take Mount Gerizim?" asks Gaius while his lecherous greedy eyes fall upon the young woman who sits down with the young lady to watch and listen.

"To invent a new Messiah," adds Pontius as he notes this hearing is very much a means by which Gaius will establish himself as the star act.

The Senator nods at Caligula for approval and walks up to Pontius. Senator Vinicianus was close to Tiberius and not one of Gaius's men. Vinicianus has transposed his loyalty, from the late Caesar, to the early Caesar, a political move for self-preservation. Wisely he places himself near to Caligula for this protection, for an evaluation of his rule and observations that may expose his risk to the dangers inherent in this young man.

Vinicianus attempts to distract Gaius by introducing Yeshua. He will attempt to show that Pontius was often redirected. This intended means to defend Pontius is also an attempt to test his own ability to influence the young Caesar.

"The holy man: Was he not the one you had crucified?"

Gaius has heard and asks, "Yeshua the teacher?" Caligula, as Apollo, puts down the harp and brandishes a bow and an arrow.

"That incident was several years before the Samaritan revolt," Pontius wonders why Vinicianus has raised the matter and confused the two self-proclaimed messiahs?

Caligula aims his arrow at the two fearful females: He fires and misses on purpose. They flinch. He puffs his chest.

Gaius pronounces unconvincingly. "We will establish the Prefect of Judea used his high rank to murder the Samaritans and the Yehudim, that teacher for one."

His patience falters with this pathetic display of legal amateurisms, Pontius blurts, "Rebellions removed with military force are not murders!"

Caligula aims his next arrow at Pontius. "But you did knowingly crucify an innocent man." Not intimidated, Pontius does not waver. He ignores the remark. Vinicianus remains silent giving way to Pontius's testimony, his own best means of defense.

"I would be fighting an ever-growing, even-stronger force of resistance to the Roman Empire had I not done so."

Caligula as 'Apollo' raises another arrow and aims to threaten. "Vinicianus. Our brave Prefect has a sound reason. To slay the Samaritans. He also prevented a revolt against the building of aqueducts. Something for their own good. The crucifixion of the teacher needs to be considered. But was this also murder? The willful killing of an innocent man: To prevent an escalation of hostility against our empire?"

"Yeshua of Nazareth refused to denounce his claim to be king ..."

"Stop!" Caligula pulls the string of the bow, keeps his aim at Pontius.

Pontius takes heed when interrupted by the ruler of Rome who points the arrow. Tension on the bow: Hand quivering, fires the arrow misses Pontius by inches. Thud! Gaius is a circus act without rehearsals. "We will not discuss this now!" Caligula moves and whispers to Vinicianus.

"Senator, let us not be in haste to prosecute the Prefect." He leaves hurriedly, grabs the giggling young lady by the hand as he goes.

"Remain under house arrest." Vinicianus orders Pontius to do so.

From the mood of the foregoing fracas Pontius's perceptions indicate a protracted debate with Gaius. The Prefect sees exhibitionism, recklessness and folly are all the traits of youth. Wisdom and leniency come with maturity.

Pontius turns to exit and walks with the two Praetorian Guards who informally escort him through the palace. As he walks along the wide opulent corridor passing statues, Dominicus appears, a matured young woman and mother. She looks at Pontius intent and surprised but silent. A ten-year-old girl, Gina, holds her hand. Pontius stops involuntarily. The two Guards halt also. Giana asks, "Who's that?"

Memories of Dominicus's affection for him flood his brain with a twinge of guilt. Dominicus keeps walking passed him as he swivels to follow her line of path. She looks back over her shoulder and nods twice, an affirmation to confirm his thoughts about the girl. Impotency eradicated as his mind turns to curiosity. But this opportunity disappears behind closed doors. He has no desire to reenter.

Outside the palace Claudia waits faithfully. The Guard duty terminates here. Pontius embraces her.

THE MAUSOLEUM OF AUGUSTUS

Senators Vinicianus and Aquila, with stealth, search, enter a corridor and around a curved wall inside the Mausoleum of Augustus late at night. Out of the darkness, two uniformed figures step from a vaulted chamber, Tribunes Chaerea and Sabinus meet Vinicianus and Aquila. The Tribunes draw them into the chamber for discussions.

PONTIUS'S VILLA

Claudia and Pontius sit despondent in their villa. Claudia turns and embraces him. She rubs his back, his stomach, and strokes his legs. He rouses, caresses, they kiss. She leads him away.

Later, Claudia and Pontius, mellow, post coital, reenter the main reception area. Pontius's mind, clouds with thoughts of Dominicus and his daughter. He restrains himself from a confession while at the same time anxious to explain that Claudia must be barren. He loves Claudia. He cannot destroy her trust in him. He cannot divulge what he knows. He wonders what has been gained by using Dominicus for his own experimentation.

"What are you thinking about?" Claudia can sense something.

In the interlude Centurion Antonius has arrived and refills his goblet. A sympathetic observer he feels an oppressive atmosphere.

Claudia looks to her husband who offers, "We wait."

They are housebound waiting on Gaius to reopen the case against Pontius.

Antonius asks, "What else can we do?" He looks to Claudia, his cousin.

"We can flee" she says boldly.

"Gaul?" suggests Antonius.

While Claudia offers "Britannia?"

"Rome reaches everywhere."

Senator Vinicianus enters Pontius's villa. He holds various scrolls, led by Shira. Claudia looks upon him anxiously. Pontius gestures for him to sit down. Shira leaves with a sideways glance at Antonius. He catches a glimpse of her but believes his thoughts are wishful.

"Are you summoned here by Caligula?" asks Claudia.

Vinicianus shakes his head, "No. The Emperor prefers the company of his horse to his Senate or even you!"

Claudia's anxiety rings in with a clang, "The waiting is interminable. Our lives are stagnant. Pontius has nothing to do but recount his actions. Everything my husband has done has been above reproach."

She observes in him a very quiet mood. She suspects a condition that might be called situational melancholia.

Shira returns and offers goblets of water all around. Antonius exchanges his empty goblet for a full one. Shira casts her eyes down so as not to make eye contact with him.

The Senator takes some refreshing water from Shira. "Caligula has a noble project, like you once had in Jerusalem; building two new aqueducts for Rome." He looks to Pontius who remains quiet. "The Senate knew you killed all the Yehudim who opposed your aqueducts."

Anxiously Claudia offers, "Oh, more accusers!" The wait takes a toll on the nerves and sanity of the sane.

Vinicianus remains close to the Emperor as a means of protection and preservation. "Gaius Caligula is obsessively competitive. If anyone challenges his abilities, and he thinks he has many, or if they possess skills greater than his own, they are soon disposed of, thrown to the lions to save the costs of buying their food."

Claudia interjects an accusation. "The Tribune should be on trial here." A reference to the way her husband's orders were misused during the attack on the Samaritans at Mount Gerizim. The Tribune took an order of containment to extreme; an out-and-out eradication of the retreating Samaritans. Pontius honorably accepts his responsibility while Claudia defends his reputation.

"Any criticism of Caligula's theatrics, or failing to swear to his genius, he will have his victims placed in a tight cage and sawn in half." Vinicianus imparts as a caution not to be drawn into the Emperor's trap.

Pontius, recognizes the futility of his hope, turns it into a joke. "So, I'll not be given the job to build his aqueducts?"

"He plays with you." The senator has had conversations with Gaius and makes no progress. "The horse he loves would do a better job than you!"

Both men laugh.

Claudia says, with serious import, "If you build it well, you will steal his glory. If you build it badly, you will be to blame."

Claudia turns her palms up to Vinicianus.

"Am I to be imprisoned in my own house forever?"

Vinicianus adds as a cautionary prediction, "There's no sport in that for Caligula."

THE PALACE OF GAIUS CALIGULA

The statuesque groom stands next to a beautiful white stallion, Go-Go. The horse has eye make-up, jewels and sequins adorn his purple blanket. The mane is braided with gold wire, his legs and tail are wrapped in solid gold wire, and white fur covers his hoofs to match the plume of white feathers on his head. Two slaves stand-by ready to remove any excreta that may be deposited on the marble floor.

Decorated sumptuously, Caligula's palace is alive with the dignitaries of Rome, who are a mixture of socialites, generals and politicians, some of whom are there by intimidation and command but not preference. He mixes pleasure with an anxious wariness. This banquet includes Pontius, Claudia, and Senator Vinicianus, who sit together. Mus stands behind his master, Pontius. Mus is there by the insistence of Claudia. Despite Mus being a diminutive person, Claudia knows his loyalty to the family, and he offers protection.

Dominicus sits with Gaius's sister Livilla, speaking in hushed tones as they look toward Claudia who remains unaware of their focus. Separated a safe distance from Pontius, they discuss the likelihood that his wife is barren.

"They have no children," Dominicus informs Livilla. She has never revealed to anyone that her daughter was sired by Pontius.

Nearby, Anicius Cerealis, father, and his son, Sextus Papinius view the proceedings with caution. Unfortunately, Sextus's good looks will draw the attention of the other handsome ladies away from Gaius.

Gnaeus Dominitius Ahenobarbus arrives late. Dominicus's husband, a stern-faced man, violent by nature, approaches Dominicus. "Gina needs you home now."

"She is not alone."

"Let's get out of here now!"

They leave. Gnaeus pushes Dominicus firmly ahead directing her out. As they do so, Dominicus looks toward Pontius. He returns her gaze. Claudia catches his line-of-sight who may only wonder about the woman he sees but says nothing.

Dominicus gave Pontius the double-nod to confirm his thought that Gina is his daughter. So, who is the man pushing her out of the party? Pontius assumes Gnaeus is her husband. The attitude Gnaeus displays toward Dominicus, just in that moment, appears less than tender.

The music continues. Caligula, the tragic-comic, hideous in dark make-up, wears a sinister black costume with decorations. He dances around the floor, a man possessed, a primitive ballet-like animation: Perfect in ugliness! He beckons for someone to join him. He makes his way through the guests. All are fearful. No one offers.

The emperor god zeros in on Claudia, who freezes. His ballet takes on the stealth of a snake. He grabs both her hands, pulls her onto the floor violently and pulls her shockingly close into him, forces her to move erotically. Pontius grips his own legs to restrain himself. Mus notices. Claudia starts to respond to his dance by innovative moves that fit the progression in the hope to appease him. Then she realizes her dilemma. He views this as a submission and for compliance. She reverts quickly to a fearful stone-like-paralysis.

Caligula notices her passion has gone, pushes her backwards across to a table. Terror on her face makes him smile like a beast. With total disregard for any decorum whatsoever, he rips at her garments with the frenzy of a hideous hyena, ignoring her screams.

The musicians stop playing. The guests are aghast. She fights back flailing at him with all her might. Gaius becomes aroused, erotically charged to play along instead of proceeding with a direct rape.

Anicius Cerealis and his son Sextus Papinius focus on a restrained Pontius and look to him to take action to protect his wife's virtue: Pontius strategizes and whispers to Mus.

Claudia fights with Caligula who relishes the battle willing to make more entertainment out of it. He waves at the musicians to start-up again, which they do. The guests look on, silent.

Suddenly the horse rears-up neighing, spooked as Mus who emerges from the other side of the animal and scampers out before being seen. Caligula's groom holds the horse down. Caligula looks to his horse, suddenly abandons Claudia and runs to the groom, beats him furiously.

Claudia, torn clothes, disheveled, runs to meet Pontius and they leave covertly with Senator Vinicianus. Mus does not escape unnoticed. Neither do Pontius, Claudia and Vinicianus get away as invisibly as they may suppose. While Caligula comforts Go-Go, like he might console his lover, his beady eyes swivel in their sockets to see the escaping party. The band plays on.

Caligula hands the reins back to his groom, walks to Anicius and Sextus, and looks at them terrifyingly to take extra interest in Sextus. He smiles, turns to his audience and encourages their applause. Slowly at first, building up a roar of approval, clapping hands, cheers, to make it appear his performance was a complete success.

ROME'S STREETS

The ominous dark streets of Rome, a cool reminder, their ordeal is not over, they have not really escaped. Vinicianus hurries along with Claudia, Pontius and Mus. They see Senator Aquila and Tribunes Chaerea and Sabinus emerge from the darkness. Vinicianus stops; looks to Pontius. Odious, silent, the Tribunes wait for a cue. Pontius stares at Vinicianus who merely states one name to explain everything.

"Caligula."

Pontius 'studies' the group. "Do not inform me of anything Caligula would want to know."

"We need your tactical advice, militarily speaking."

Vinicianus insists, as if that is the only requirement of him. Claudia still disheveled and recovering slowly, looks at Pontius long-contemplating and awaiting his response.

In the vacuum she sees her husband's uncertainty, offers them, "Will you come with us?"

"Thank you" Vinicianus nods to move them along.

Pontius and Claudia hasten into the darkness. She leads the way. Taking advantage of the impersonal nature of the blackness of the night she broaches the subject, "Who was that woman?'

"Which woman?"

"You know."

"The one leaving with her escort?"

"Yes."

"You may have seen her before Claudia."

"Me?"

"She was in the crowd the day we left Rome for Judea, ten years ago."

"Who is she?"

"I'll tell you when I am ready."

Vinicianus cannot avoid overhearing the prickly conversation.

19

TORTURE

DUNGEONS

Silent prisoners depleted of life languish in the dungeons. Sack cloth drapes over human formations. It is hard to see if they are dead or alive? Smoking torches ensconced to the walls burn to light the torture chamber, but the shadows depressingly dominate the dimness. The atmosphere ominous, the odors of an animal circus pervade the air. An elephant trumpet blasts and echoes around the cavern. A lion roars to add chills.

Dark and dank below ground a small group of Roman noblemen and women, including father and son, Anicius and Sextus, huddle together quietly. They are being subjected to a command performance as an audience intimidated to attend for fear their absence would incur their arrest. Reluctant to endorse the antics of the tyrannically insane they are nonetheless in captivity too. Caligula has the ability to harness his invisible reign of terror.

Within the audience one man appears out of context. He appears wearing civilian clothes never seen wearing before now. He lingers in the background, alone. His eyes identify his dark soul. To gain anonymity, Centurion Lefus, once loyal to Pontius, who made a protracted withdrawal of his respect for the Prefect, and turned spy.

Enter the Emperor with his Praetorian Guard, eight tall, heavy-set men. As usual, theatrical in a hideous costume, his make-up, weapons, intends to look intimidating; if Caligula were not so clownish. Some in the small crowd dare to snigger, then quickly stifle a snort and remove their smile. "You are all witnesses!" Caligula exclaims. He intends his observers to be frightened out of any notion that might make them think they can conspire against him. He orders the removal of the first sackcloth. "The extraction of the truth," he announces.

Mus, tied to a rack lies on his back; four big gladiator types hold his reins slack, his body taught with fear and his face strained in muted silence. Caligula looks greedily toward Sextus to impress him with his power. Gaius would have him intuitively understand that power is more attractive than beauty. Then with a flourish he points to another cloth like an apprentice magician. "A witness to the truth," he boasts.

Second, he removes the cloth draped over an individual standing against the wall. Shira, her arms and legs spread: Her wrists and ankles shackled to the wall, she perspires profusely, shakes uncontrollably. He announces his prizes. "The conspirators!" and with a flurry he pulls the sack cloth off Pontius and Claudia who sit on a stone with no backrest. They are humiliatingly held in place with ankle shackles and a heavy log anchored across their legs.

Caligula approaches his crowd. "This equestrian, this Prefect of Judea and Samaria, executed an innocent, harmless, Yehudim teacher, Yeshua." He turns around to face Pontius and Claudia. "Whose only crime was to imagine himself a king. The Prefect stole Temple funds and killed those who objected: Hundreds of innocent people. He massacred a village of Samaritan men, women and children: Thousands upon thousands of harmless, unarmed peasants. His latest and greatest crime! To plot against me! Me! Gaius Caesar, your emperor, your god." He beckons applause, smiles, revels in his own show.

Claudia whispers to Pontius, "Our God is YeHoVaH the Father of Yeshua."

Pontius looks at Claudia blankly. "Are we Hebrews now?"

Caligula abruptly turns back to Pontius. "Give me the names of those who are plotting with you." He leans in closer. "I will set you, your wife and your household free."

Fearless, Pontius looks straight into his eyes. "You have wrongly judged me guilty on three counts. You may execute me only once."

"Not so hasty Pilatus," Caligula uses the familiar Latin 'Pilatus' in an attempt at endearment. "Three of your households are here." He spins and gestures broadly, "They will give me the names."

"They have no names to give you."

"Ahhh but we shall find out."

"You would add three innocent people to the many hundreds of people who lost their lives under my rule?" Caligula jumps around Mus like a cat plays, "Ah ha! A confession: You murdered many hundreds of people?"

"Would Rome confess to the killing of many thousands of people to acquire and protect our empire? I have done nothing less than Rome would do!"

The crowd hums warmly. Faces in the crowd take on a serious look.

"He is clever, isn't he!?" Caligula encourages them nodding to agree with him. "Pilatus thinks I will pardon him. Look how confident, how smug he is. Do you know why?" He shakes his head from side to side to encourage the crowd to follow him. "He believes he saved my life when I fell from my horse." He turns to face Pontius. "I was saved by my fellow gods Neptune, Mercury and Jupiter to fulfil my destiny to be your Emperor, your god!" Claudia cannot contain herself in silence any longer. "My husband saved you and you know it. You are nothing." Pontius tries to quiet her by digging his elbow into her side.
"But sick and vile like your uncle." Pontius closes his eyes in defeat. Surprisingly restrained, Caligula smiles, "And this is how you repay my husband? The man who did save your life!"

A deathly hush pervades. Caligula plays with the silence. He turns inward. Loudly Gaius proclaims, "There is enough anger there to want to kill me!" He looks around those gathered. "Who else is in this plot?" Then stares down on Claudia, "Give me their names!"

"Who would *not* want you dead?"

The preposterousness of such a claim leaves Gaius totally stumped.

Caligula goes to Mus and opens his arms, fingers pointed in opposing directions, orders the Gladiators to stretch him. Pain registers on Mus' face, he puffs/breathes air but no sound, no cries, no pleading for mercy? "Little man, who else is in this plot? Tell us or we will stretch you to full length. To normal height: How long would you like to be?"

Pontius shouts, "He's mute, he can't speak."

Caligula motions the gladiators to stop and untie Mus. "Ha ha ha ha. Of course, of course, my aunt could not let him speak of her many lovers." His hollow eyes gaze upon Anicius Cerealis and his son Sextus Papinius. He approaches them. "You didn't remind me the mouse has no squeak." He beckons them to step forward. Anicius and Sextus tremble.

Anicius, with obvious fear, "We didn't know, just like you."

"Of course, I knew you idiot!" The Emperor waves at Mus to come forward. Awkwardly and painfully, he limps to Caligula. Caligula prances around as if he has the mouse in his mouth.

"Ahhhhh yes, formerly my Aunt Julia's dwarf," With an attempt at charm, "My aunt had many lovers." Gaius was a boy at the time, but he remembers his aunt had a fetish for dwarfs. He suspects Mus fulfilled the role of servant in many ways not least of all perhaps personal services.

"You may have the honor Mus. Pick father or son?" Mus hesitates, he has no idea what he is being honored for. He looks to Caligula seeking direction. Caligula's eyes dance feverishly at Sextus. Obeying the implied command, Mus points at Sextus. Gaius immediately moves toward Anicius.

His father Anicius suspects punishment, foul play and circus entertainment, none of which is justified for such a slight infraction, the omission that Mus is mute. "No. My son is…"

Shock registers on Anicius' face before he can complete his sentence with the word "innocent". He slumps to the ground. Caligula pulls the bloodied dagger out of Anicius' abdomen. The crowd gasps. Caligula motions to the gladiators to grab a stunned Sextus.

"Pull him to pieces!"

Claudia grabs the hand of Pontius and holds it behind the stone they sit upon.

Caligula turns to the crowd. "Anicius Cerealis, you were executed this day for plotting against the Emperor of Rome."

Mus aches, sits down, lies down.

The gladiators pull the ropes tied to Sextus who screeches in pain. Caligula motions to the prone Mus to applaud. He then turns to the crowd and works them up into a frenzy of applause. The volume of the applause drowns out the cries of Sextus who falls unconscious. Pontius motions Claudia to remain silent.

"Stop!" Unpredictable, Gaius walks over to Shira, shows her his bloodied dagger and places the blade between her legs. She shudders with fear, tears stream down her face. He looks around at Claudia and smirks, goading her to object to his treatment of Shira but she remains silent. He looks at Pontius.

He forcefully says to Shira, "Look at me! I am your master, your superior, your god, not him." Sextus moans.

"Rome pays too much for animal food. Put Sextus in the cage with the lions."

The gladiators drag Sextus away.

He delights in preying on the most fearful. Pontius will offer a challenge, resistance, he would prefer to delay. The weak are the best means by which to find out the secrets of the strong. "Who shall we feed to the lions tomorrow? You? What may be left of you?" He allows Shira time to consider her fate. "Name the senators who have been to the Prefect's villa."

Shira, shakes uncontrollably, appears to be totally broken. "Vinicianus." At this Caligula is pleasingly surprised. Then Shira ads, "Ordered there by you your excellency, Emperor of Rome." Caligula looks quite pleased; presses his lips together in a condescending manner to conceal anger at the contempt she shows toward him. He removes the threat of the dagger.

Trying to turn this to his success he says, "That was easy. Who else?"

Shira replies with newly summoned courage. "No one your Excellency; the Prefect has no friends."

Amused, Gaius is taken by surprise at her fortitude to stand up to him. "Ah Ha Humm." He even deigns to laugh a little. "The truth!"

At the back of the audience Lefus takes vicarious delight to watch Shira being intimidated by the crazy emperor.

His fantasies near realization, the vulnerable bound Shira could be ravaged by Lefus. He sweats with sadistic lust.

Without warning Caligula moves toward Pontius brutally smashes him in the face with the butt of his bloody dagger. Pontius falls backwards dazed and strained; no back rest to the stone they sit upon. His ankles chafe in the irons, his weight pulls up under the log across his thighs. Pontius groans. Claudia twists in her restraints and lifts him back up.

In a moment Gaius has transformed himself from snake to tiger. The madness of paranoia not without some foundation, "You, an insignificant equestrian," he plays to the crowd. "His whore and his little household of deformed and degenerate servants mean nothing to me!" He devalues life and screams at Pontius, "Give me the names of the men plotting against me!!!" Claudia who has nothing to mop up with except her hands hesitatingly gives careful attention to Pontius's wound not wishing to agitate it.

He composes himself and with amazing political aplomb. "Your uncle Tiberius Caesar handled the threat yet remained emperor for twenty-three years."

Caligula, amused, prances in front of the crowd, returns to his snake-like nature, "Listen to how he avoids a simple question."

"This is the answer. Your uncle lived and ruled from the island of Capreae."

"What is your point Pilatus?"

"Live in private seclusion only seeing those you want to see. Your alleged assassins cannot reach you there. It will be safe."

Caligula sniggers awkwardly and smiles. "You're distracting me Prefect. It isn't safe there."

Pontius succeeds in exposing Caligula. "So, you do know that?!"

Pontius now has his full attention.

"Everyone knows my uncle died of natural causes."

"Or was someone instructed to suffocate your uncle?"

Gentle snoring heard: Caligula looks around the dungeon to see Mus lying flat on his back. "Ah ha, the mouse speaks through his nose." Caligula laughs and encourages his entourage, so they all laugh in feigned and fearful respect in contrast to Pontius who, while bruised and bloodied, remains in perceived authority.

Suddenly a lion's roar and a human scream. Sextus cries out for mercy but he is ignored. "If I feed your mouse to the lions, will we hear him scream too?"

"There's not enough meat on a small mouse to satisfy a big cat."

Caligula enjoys the banter. Then suddenly, without warning, screams at Pontius! "I am your god!" Caligula places the bloodied dagger across Pontius's throat. "Tell me the truth! Am I your god?!!! Tell me it is true!!! I am your true god!!! Me. Gaius Caesar, your emperor, your god."

Claudia whispers, "Yeshua." Pontius motions Caligula to come even closer. Pontius whispers. Caligula listens.

"Yeshua of Nazareth, Ha'netzaeret, The King of the Yehudim said," Pontius pauses, "'everyone who is of the truth hears my voice.'"

Caligula frowns. Whatever Pontius means, eludes him. Spiritual deafness, within the darkness of the emperor's soul, lurks there, unwilling to release him from bondage.

Blinding lightening crackles enters the torture chamber and dungeon to over-expose the scene. Caligula flinches. The ground shakes! The thunder deafens everyone. Caligula removes the dagger from Pontius' throat.

Mus, with aching limbs, struggles to his feet as Shira stands free of her manacles, which have mystically fallen away, giving her great relief, freedom. Caligula stares at her incredulously. She inscribes letters in the dusty soil, Y H V H and vocalizes "Yeshua Ha'netzaeret V' melek Ha' Yehudim." Meaning, "Yeshua of Nazareth King of the Jews." More lightning, shuddering and thunder follow in close succession.

Pontius sees Caligula in a state of indecision, so he orders him, "Your horse, Go-Go!" Mus nods approval.

Vinicianus appears. Caligula points to Pontius and Claudia. "Vinicianus! Sport, for another day!" With a maniacal laugh Caligula leaves, motions to his Praetorian Guard and they follow hurriedly. The crowd hurriedly exits and scatters.

Vinicianus unshackles Pontius and Claudia. He removes the heavy wood from across their thighs. Claudia embraces her husband. They regain some circulation in their legs by rubbing their thighs. The thunder rumbles ominously. The senator predicts, "A storm, torrential rain, go home. I will come to see you," and exits in haste.

Relieved, they stand, stiff, gradually straighten their knees, cling to one another. Slowly at first, Pontius pulsates to release the tension. His eyes water, then flow with refreshment. An internalized departure from worry and danger has eradicated his fears. He has put up a formidable act of courage to face the evil of a man possessed. Claudia may be pleased she senses another transformation in him has begun as he dared whisper the name "Yeshua" as if to invoke the mystical power of YeHoVaH, that huge clap of thunder.

Dominicus, beaten and bruised, suddenly appears with Gina.

She looks to Claudia. "Please, if anything happens to me look after Gina."

"Who are you?"

Pontius waits apprehensively while Dominicus calculates her reply.

"A friend."

"Why not her father?"

"Yes." Dominicus looks to Pontius.

The dawn rises on Claudia very slowly.

"But who was the man with you at the palace?"

"My husband Gnaeus. Gina was three years old when we married. He never accepted her. Jealous, he tried to hit her, but I wouldn't let him."

"Look at our situation with Caligula. He could have killed *us now here* today!"

"I know, I have begged my brother not to harm you. He won't, he just wants to know who is conspiring to kill him."

"Look what he has done to my husband!" The

dusk falls on Claudia slowly.

"Maybe you are right my brother wants to banish me."

Claudia's dark thoughts cloud over. She looks to the child.

"I know you are a good woman, Claudia. Please bring up Gina as your own."

Dominicus begins to shake bodily, her face torn, her eyes full of tears. "I know you will make a good mother. Take her now. Escape."

Claudia's intuition confirms her suspicion. She looks intently at Pontius and asks pointedly, "Gina is your daughter?"

Pontius concedes this day of shocks without a word. His bruised and bloody face doubles as an acknowledgment of responsibility for Gina, with shame.

Claudia looks to Pontius who hastens to say with urgency, "Let's get away from this place." Pontius cannot take his gaze away from Gina. Claudia has apoplexy, her feet feel riveted to the ground. He grabs Claudia and Gina by joining their hands. He motions Dominicus to follow. Gina looks over her shoulder at her mother who in a state of near emotional collapse picks up speed to be swept along in their wake.

Pontius rationalized his affair with Dominicus many years before. His intent was to discover if indeed he was impotent, unable to procreate. He did not inform Claudia to protect her from distress on more than one level. Was it a worthwhile medical experiment? Would Claudia approve of an experiment to prove she was barren? Would Claudia sanction an affair to have a child by surrogate means? He deprived Claudia the answers. He appears guilty, a philanderer. Now he can do nothing with the information. He has a daughter. Whatever way it will be played out, injured and threatened by Gaius Caligula, Pontius has another reason to live. Gina.

20
ASSASSINATION

January 41 AD

Caligula's unstable mental condition works within its own intelligence. To use Pontius to reveal those who may be conspiring against him, he gives him freedom. In this way Gaius believes he will draw his opponents into the open. Or at least expose them to his form of mental torture. He does just that, giving them a false sense of minor discomfort by inviting them to see him perform acts of sadism.

THE THEATER

Costumed hideously, Caligula dominates the stage of a small amphitheater for a daytime performance. He struts from character to character striking each one with his sword, drawing blood, inflicting minor injuries on everyone as they cringe. They fall, as if mortally wounded, releasing fake blood across the stage. He raises his arms in victory. Then bows.

In stunned silence, the audience waits. Among them, Claudia and Pontius watch in awesome fear and loathing. His facial injuries are less now with the lapse of healing time. Some peace in the form of a reprieve has endured this time of his recuperation. Pontius still wears the mental bruises and scars of his torture, but he has gained some sense of the divine. This sense may vacillate as he considers the place he finds he cannot escape from and they remain at the mercy of the evil emperor.

Claudia leans over to Pontius, "Let's get out of here."
Caligula straightens himself, and gestures; the audience rises and feebly begins to applaud him. They are well trained but make him demand it of them. The slow applause causes Caligula to work up to a frenzy of arm waving until the level reaches his approval.

Pontius applauds, looks anxiously at Claudia to join him but she refuses. Gaius focuses on Claudia who remains brazen despite the dangers. Then Caligula stops everyone clapping. He focuses on Claudia and Pontius. He saves face, bows and leaves the stage, stage left.

From the portico seen in the distance, young performers from Asia, rehearse ballet war-dances. People move about spilling out of the theater. In a tight corridor, a receiving line awaits, many scores of people, are expected to pander to the emperor.

The Praetorian Guard, his personal bodyguard, the hefty Germanic types who stand by, wait for the emperor: Caligula appears, no longer in costume, but resplendent in the finery of the god he thinks he is. His young wife Caesonia, and his four-year-old daughter Drusilla, walk into the
'reception' line; the crowd bows in fearful respect, closing behind the emperor, ominously.

His Guard, hindered by the reception line, linger, hesitant, curious, watch. In the receiving line, Pontius and Claudia stand motionless as Caligula, his wife and daughter approach. Pontius bows but Claudia obstinately refuses, ignores Pontius who tugs her hand to comply.

Caligula stares right into Claudia's defiant eyes. He then looks toward Pontius.

"Your whore refuses to respect me?" he screams and veins strain to burst through his neck. Caligula turns to his Praetorian Guard who is distant. He singles out one ordinary soldier who is closer to him. He points to the Roman Tribune Chaerea who is in disguise as a mismatched Praetorian Guard. "Give me your sword. Now!" he shouts. Chaerea does not mirror the appearance of the Germanic guard, pushes through slowly and keeps looking around. "What are you waiting for?" as Gaius looks also to the Germanic Praetorian guard who jostle forward against resistance. Caligula looks around. Chaerea steps closer to Caligula who pulls the sword from Chaerea's sheath, raises it toward Claudia to strike her. Pontius grabs the arm of Caligula. They struggle.

He screams, "Arrest this man!" Pontius keeps hold on him for fear that if he lets him go, he has placed himself in an impossible dilemma. They struggle awkwardly. With or without a weapon Pontius appears to want to minimize any harm. Locked in defense mode, he waits. What does he know? Caesonia picks up her daughter Drusilla.

Disarmed, Chaerea keeps looking around for someone.

Again, "What are you waiting for?" Caligula demands "Kill him! Kill him! Kill him!"

The Germanic Praetorian guard push harder more hurriedly against the reception line: Many scores of people push still harder against their advance. They try to run away in fear of what may become a hysterical riot. Bodies lock against bodies. Will against will. Kill or be killed.

"Idiot! Let me go! Kill him! Kill him!"

Chaerea looks around, fearful, apoplectic, scans the jostling crowd, one wonders what Chaerea could be waiting for, accomplices?

Caligula struggles with Pontius. The crowd hinders the Germanic Praetorian Guard progress. "Let me go you fool! Let me go!" He screams at Chaerea again, "Kill him! Kill him! Kill him!"

At last, Vinicianus, Sabinus and Aquila appear. They run from various directions. Chaerea sees them! Turbulent and vexed, Chaerea draws his dagger and stabs Caligula in the neck up through his jaw. Chillingly painful screeching noises issue forth.

Pontius pulls free as Caligula grabs his own bloodied neck and gurgles, "You! You!"

Caesonia screams! Gaius sinks to the ground.

The Germanic Praetorian guard flails at those in their way as they make slow progress forward. Caesonia, frozen in fear, hugs her child Drusilla closer.

Pontius grabs Claudia and they move quickly toward the least resistance, the ballet dancers.

Vinicianus appears from the direction of the dancers, rushes past Pontius and Claudia. Vinicianus steps forward to lean over and stab Caligula. Chaerea sees the Germanic Praetorian Guard advance, taps Vinicianus and flees.

An unidentified woman wrestles the shocked and screaming Drusilla away from Caesonia and runs away. Sabinus rushes in, stabs Caesonia and Caligula repeatedly in frenzy. She falls beside her husband.

In the melee Aquila arrives to plunge his sword into Caligula to deliver the final fatal blow. Caligula has been stabbed thirty times. Blood from "Little Boots" and Caesonia floods the area. The Germanic Praetorian guard reaches the dead bodies, fight off the crowd who stampede in panic, which pushes left and right, to run. Centurion Lefus appears to join the guards. He has chosen the opposite side to the assassins courting favor for promotion and the downfall of Pontius.

Vinicianus, Sabinus and Aquila scatter; escape. Pontius and Claudia run through the stunned, motionless ballet dancers, in haste to getaway. They all disappear in the chaotic rush to avoid the blades of the Praetorian Guard. Outnumbered, failure to defend Caligula raises their frustration. Despite his claim, the emperor's immortality as a divine being, he has died a mortal human being. This death has secured some future for Pontius and Claudia, temporarily but for how long?

21
SAVIOR

PONTIUS'S VILLA

Their villa provides little security, unlike a fortress, no defenses against any attack, no strength in construction for warfare. Claudia prepares their bed for the night.

"What are we doing!?" She asks of herself. "I must be fooling myself."

"Will the next emperor put me through this again and again?" Pontius questions.

"And now we must harbor a fugitive wife and mother *and your* daughter!"

Claudia realizes the ridiculousness of their situation. They have just left the scene of an assassination. She has had the most profound shock that her husband had an affair with Dominicus and produced a daughter he knew nothing about.

She craves the idea of escape. "We must flee to Aquitania or Narbonensis, Gaul or even Britannia!"

Relief of the threat from Caligula becomes overshadowed, replaced by the likelihood of reprisals from others. Ominous, the events of the day are far from over.

Suddenly on cue, loud knocks, Claudia jerks, "Oh no," with the uncertainty of who might be calling. A suspicion of the worst kind, for justice or revenge?

Pontius knows he cannot escape easily. While maintaining he did not want to be an assassin he is implicated as a willing accomplice, the decoy the conspirators hoped for and got. He quickly buckles his belt, sheathes his sword, ready. More knocks. An attacker would hardly be so polite. "Wait" unable to offer any relief to Claudia, he hurries from the bed chamber.

In the reception room Mus stands alert and armed, at the door. Even louder knocks prompt Pontius to nod at Mus who then unbolts the door; simultaneously Pontius draws his sword. Vinicianus, Sabinus and Aquila, armed, enter on an edge of heightened anxiety. Pontius motions to Mus to shut the door. Antonius squeezes in behind them.

Dominicus and Gina appear anxious to push in past Mus. This effectively distracts Mus who fails to re-bolt it. Countermanding the order to "wait" Claudia enters the room to stand behind her husband.

"We hope to quiet the senate," Vinicianus offers with uncertainty. Shira apprehensively appears but stays in the background.

"Will his successor pursue my husband?"

Sabinus answers, "If Claudius succeeds Caligula, who knows?"

Aquila adds, "Vitellius, The Legate of Syria, was a childhood friend of Caligula."

Resonating with this Vinicianus confirms, "And he will want to see his friend Caligula complete the work which he cannot do now."

"Claudius, assuming he succeeds, will learn that Pontius took no steps to defend Caligula," Sabinus offers skeptically.

"We put you in a defenseless position, guilty by association with us. Vitellius lusts for power. We must consider leaving, now. I do not think we can delay." Such is the gravity of their predicament as Vinicianus expresses it.

Dominicus and Gina remain mere observers while they wait in a constant state of fear and foreboding not knowing their future. Shira stands around in uncertainty waiting for direction.

The assembled gathering of conspirators in this one place can hardly help Pontius's position and their convergence will be to find a collaborative means of escape.

Sabinus, curiously is the first to ask, "Why didn't you run a blade through Caligula?"

Pontius, lost for an explanation, becomes as apoplectic as he was when he had the chance to cut Caligula down. Claudia's intuition comes forth.

"My husband experienced something inner personal. He did not want to crucify The Rabbi Yeshua. He was forced to do so. Since then he has struggled with his conscience."

Aquila astonished, "Whatever that means?"

Defending him, "It means the soul of a pagan is being changed," Antonius's belief has the ability to discern.

"What sort of crap is that centurion?" Aquila looks nervously, strung-out, ready for a fight.

"We must flee," Claudia says on cue, but it is too late.

Suddenly: The door crashes open: Centurion Lefus leads the Germanic Praetorian guard, eight of them, push their way in, plus Gnaeus who seeks out his target, Dominicus and the daughter he thinks is his own.

Mus trampled, falls backwards, cracks his head on the hard, tiled floor and falls unconscious.

Pontius shouts at Claudia. "Run!" Claudia grabs Shira's hand and tugs her, runs to the garden. Instinctively Dominicus and Gina run to follow them. Gnaeus sees his wife and daughter flee out of the room.

The outnumbered Roman men draw their swords. The earth trembles. Dust falls like rain. The dry sprinkle descends gently on Pontius as a minor distraction. He looks up but for less than a second. Lightening cracks and flashes: Thunder claps: The building fractures. A gap appears in the masonry.

Gnaeus ducks and dives around the battle to follow the women into the garden.

Just inside the door, Mus stirs, silent, shaken by the moving earth, the mosaic tiles around him crack and splinter. His eyes come into focus to survey the scene. This offers him a moment to strategize. Chaerea appears in the doorway, nods an acknowledgement at Mus, a silent indication, a partnership, in arms.

Lefus attacks Antonius. Shocked the man whom he worked alongside for so many years finally unleashes his pent-up frustrations and jealousies upon Antonius, who backs away. Lefus advances in a mad fury that nears the border of an emotional breakdown. Lefus in his neurotic outburst flails against Antonius using the limitless energy of a relentless demon. His advance as he slashes and swipes his way forces Antonius to retreat using defensive action to prevent contact. His skill running backwards, uncanny, unlike Lefus, Antonius preserves his strength.

The skilled swordsman Lefus turns into a reckless warrior, unable to focus his tactical energy. Lefus continues to use up his last bit of might as he sees he has Antonius tripping backwards.

Hand-to-hand, swords clash. Vinicianus, Sabinus and Aquila defend; flailing iron; they retreat as the German bigger men, the Praetorians advance eight against three. They push on to stampede the Romans.

Claudia, Shira, Dominicus and Gina huddle together hidden from Gnaeus. He looks around in the darkness stabbing his sword mercilessly into the undergrowth like a man possessed of madness.

Pontius rushes to join the three Romans, flails against the Praetorians, iron sparks, chops, swings, hacks, and stabs at the guards, who split to outnumber them two to one. Pontius has energy that rises to heights never attained before.

Mus rises to his feet. Chaerea waits for him to combine forces. Chaerea and Mus enter behind the Germans and attacks from the rear as does Mus. Mus swings his sword, two-handed, slices at the Achilles heel of one German who falls immobilized. Chaerea cuts his throat. The attackers only outnumber the defenders by one now and press on for a hoped advantage.

Lightning flashes: Thunder rumbles and booms. The earth trembles. Dust falls. Chunks of masonry drop. Crack! Boom! The building fractures again. Mus, mouth opens, gasps air, he speaks for the first time, "Look out!!!" That gets Antonius' attention.

Antonius falls back; Lefus advances in a frenzy in a near depleted state of diminished stamina. The earth shifts, Lefus stumbles exposed to Antonius, poised to run him through. Columns collapse. The roof falls in around them. Before Antonius can deliver a deathly penetrating counter lunge, crash, a beam falls just inches between the two centurions. Lefus disappears from Antonius's line-of-sight. The loud crash of masonry muffles the cries of Lefus and those others trapped inside under beams and plaster. The whole building has come down on assailant and defender alike.

Simultaneously in the garden the lightning flash illuminates the group of women huddled together. Gnaeus approaches swiftly and plunges his sword into the midst of them.

A dust cloud rises and falls where once stood the villa. A moment of silence arrests the unbreathable air before stirring. A powder dust of fog makes the area blind to Claudia, Dominicus, Gina and Shira who have hid in the untouched garden. Where is Gnaeus? Slow creaks. Cracks settle. Groans permeate the silence. Claudia and Shira are the first to emerge.

Mus walks out of the dust: Serene Silence.

Claudia and Shira climb on top of the rubble to inspect the damage and frantically begin to remove the fallen masonry. Vinicianus staggers up out of the rubble, stunned, cut, bleeding. Claudia sights him and scrambles over the wreckage. Mus pulls Chaerea free, with cuts, dust and bloodied grime.

Claudia calls out, "Pontius! Pontius!" Shira pulls masonry off Aquila. He stirs, sword in hand. Antonius appears, unscathed. Shira looks to the Centurion with a halting and longing concern. Sabinus lies unconscious.

"Pontius!" cries Claudia.

His voice pierces a pile of rubble. "Over here! I'm in here!"

Claudia pulls at the rubble. Shira, Antonius and Mus join in with Claudia, hands by hands full of debris, thrown aside to reveal the head, then shoulders, torso. Pontius frees his legs to emerge covered in dust but without a blemish. His hand holds an object he uses to push himself up with. Claudia hugs Pontius; puts his head in the nape of her neck and says, "We must find Gina and her mother." He drops the lead covered iron rod. The same type of seal used at the tomb of Yeshua. Has Pontius been resurrected too?

Aquila plunges his sword into the rubble: The sound of a dying Praetorian guard: Blood curdles, "Ahh!"

Pontius and Claudia walk over the rubble of the collapsed villa into the garden.

Sabinus, concussed, stirs. Chaerea, and Aquila lift Sabinus up. Chaerea climbs back up onto the rubble and plunges his sword down into the masonry several times: A groan. The trapped Praetorian Guard lie buried. They die under the weight of the collapsed building. Some Romans want to make sure.

Vinicianus rises covered in dust, coughing, rubs the grit from around his eyes.

Chaerea, Aquila, Sabinus, look around, check for the possibility of more or surviving Praetorian Guards. They scan their surrounds for any signs of another force of attack. Nothing but a peaceful panorama persists. Antonius climbs back and forth over the collapsed building, searches for survivors but all remains quiet and except his own noise, his footsteps over the lose rubble. The Romans cannot comprehend their so-called good luck, but it is in fact what Claudia and Antonius recognize as divine intervention.

It is as if the city of Rome has slept while the Unseen Visitor of the night has taken only what He wants and delivered justice for Pontius. Significantly, the surrounding villas remain intact? The survivors all move out to the garden in wonderment.

Pontius and Claudia search the dust covered garden for Dominicus. They hear muffled weeping and approach Gina who shoves and tugs at her stepfather Gnaeus as she tries to dislodge him. Dominicus lies on her back dead. Slumped motionless on top of her, Gnaeus, stab wounds in his back. Dominicus holds his dagger which protrudes from his back. Gnaeus's elbow is raised and his sword disappears into Dominicus's torso somewhere underneath him. Crying Gina pulls at her stepfather and yet she cannot shift his dead weight. Claudia reaches for Gina and encourages her to stand up.

Pontius pulls Gnaeus off Dominicus pushing him to one side. He checks Dominicus for vital signs and shakes his head at Gina. Simultaneously Claudia and Pontius embrace Gina to muffle her sobs as the little girl's arms extend around Claudia.

Pontius looks skyward and exhales. Claudia intently looks to Pontius for an expression of the relief he must feel. They continue to comfort Gina in their three-way-unbroken hug. He may ponder his good fortune to be spared by this timely intervention of nature or consider the Acts of YeHoVaH. His mind tries to grip the enormous possibilities of his wildest imaginings. With it, a sense of euphoria begins to germinate within his being.

Chaerea, Aquila, Sabinus, Vinicianus, Shira and Mus gaze astonished at their immediate surroundings, the villa laid flat. Antonius walks out. Dazed they look around.

The three-way-hug separate momentarily to survey the terrain. "A miracle" whispers Claudia but Pontius's pragmatic mind wrestles with the sights before him. Thunder rumbles in the distance and moves away. Gina holds Claudia's hand.

One handed, Claudia re-embraces Pontius who sighs again with relief. Pontius stares at the stars in the sky. Exhausted, Chaerea, Aquila, Sabinus, and Vinicianus sit down in the terraces of rubble to reflect on the enormity of what has happened. Gina continues her hold on Claudia.

Massive lightning from west to east illuminates the city to gain their attention yet again. Thunder, close at hand then the sound moves off into the distance more quickly than usual. Pontius clings to Claudia while Gina needs to hug them.

Antonius looks skyward. Shira focuses on him. He glances at her. She smiles a warm unrestrained look of interest and hope. Suddenly, out of the villa, a Pretorian guard emerges covered in dirty blood, staggers toward Antonius. He stands at the ready to wrestle him with his bare hands but the big man collapses, expires before he can reach them. Just enough momentum to propel Shira into the arms of Antonius for safety; and they giggle together in relief.

Claudia holds Pontius tight and intuitively whispers the internalized revelation from above. One word that means to save in Hebrew, "Yeshua."

The word echoes in his mind and slip from his lips. "Yeshua." Pontius recalls he pleaded with Yeshua to speak to him. So, Pilate might save him. Pontius had the power to both crucify him or release him. Pontius told him. [John 19:10] Yeshua did not defend himself. He instead said, "Thou couldest have no power *at all* against me, except it were given thee from above: therefore, he that delivered me unto thee hath the greater sin." [John 19:11]

As his mind takes him from a state of unworthiness, for all the people who have died by his order and by his hand, tears flood into his eyes and roll down his cheeks unabated. Gina senses his change and looks upon Pontius in wonderment and awe. She has never seen a man cry before. All the tension under the suppression of Caligula, all the feelings of guilt, profound regrets that have burdened his life for over a decade since he crucified Yeshua, flows down and out. From the top of his head through every bone, muscle and sinew, the molecules and atoms of his very being are flushed clean. Transforms him from a fear ridden individual, sensationally, every minuscule cell within him is renewed. The change complete, his weight lifted, intangibly disconnected from his past, he metamorphoses into a new creature of joy. Claudia feels it too.

Then with concern he ponders aloud, "I don't deserve this. How can you forgive me?"

She pulls her head back to look into his watery eyes, takes his hand, smiles, and places his hand on her stomach, nods positively. "I could not tell you before."

Pontius says, "I feel the newness of life in you, in us, remarkable, I also feel the 'newness' within me too. As if I was in a bath, but for the first time I am clean within." She smiles again as tears of joy trickle down her cheeks. They open their arms to embrace Gina who is transfixed by the atmosphere.

Dawn breaks and the boy with rosacea, now twenty-five years old, appears in the street to stop and stare at the collapsed villa.

SLOW FADE

An elderly couple approach to walk around the young man and climb over the rubble. Within moments, in haste, an even older couple arrive to climb over the destruction.

Acknowledgement Pre Script. On the 31st July 2023, my friend Mr. Trevor John Keates went home to be with Our Heavenly Father. "Special" does not adequately describe Trevor. He had brilliance in *all* areas of his life, both professional as a BAFTA Award-Winning Editor and story-teller, actor, businessman, but also as a father to two lovely children, Joseph and Ella, and devoted to his wife Jennifer. Both Jennifer and Trevor contributed so much to *Pontius Redeemed*. Jennifer is an accomplished, produced playwright, actor, businesswoman and mother. Trevor, irresistible, irreplaceable, forever missed on earth.

ACKNOWLEDGEMENTS

I wish to thank my creative team, for the contribution of their gifts and talents, for their work on the film development and this book; Arthur Donald Osborne, Susan Izdepski, Christine Harris, Caroline Slater, Montgomery Triz, Jennifer Ayres, Trevor Keates, Gruffydd Wyn Vaughan, and the late Ray Campbell.

And I would be neglectful if I did not mention my loyal patrons, Chuck Van Soye, David G. Norwood, Diane T. Covan, Dr. C. David & Barbara Jones, Ed Herider, the late Emerald Alvarez, George Cooper, Gerald A. Salerno, Jack & Linda deVore, Jeannette Saunders, Jesper Ek, Jim & Elaine Sullivan, Ellen Anastos, Arthur & Katharine Osborne, Kathleen Williams, Marissa Alvarez, Michael Zielinski, Mike Broughton, the late Ray Campbell, Raymond McKnight, the late Raymond Shockley, Robert Owen, Susan Izdepski, and Terry St Jean. Matthew Helmrich and The Helmrich foundation.

I am indebted to my readers who evaluated this book, members of the Key West Writers Guild, Edgardo Alvarado Vazquez, Rusty Hodgdon, Laura Knight, Dick Moody, Katrina Nichols, Chuck Van Soye and Judi Winters.

Plus, my appreciation for my friends and patrons, Cork Irick, Susan Izdepski, Jeff Minalga, Katharine Osborne and Michael Zielinski who read my book.

In particular I must repeat my thanks to Jeff M. and Mike Z. for their many and unlimited hours of deliberations. Susan I.

for teaching me much by bringing additional Biblical facts to my attention about which I had no previous knowledge; for being that human who accompanied YeHoVaH's messenger in the second most remarkable experience of my life. Art O. for being available every day with Biblical ideas plus his haunting film score. It was James H. Barrett who actually demanded I finish the screenplay!

Additional proof reading thanks to the very keen eyes of Barbara Jones, Beanie Kernan, Dr. C. David Jones, Linda deVore and Terry St Jean.

Finally, my new friend Katrina Nichols, my dedicated Editor-in-Chief, who checked every single word and grammatical mistake and made comments and suggestions to improve my work; yet another devout lady who believes in the sanctity of this book.

I would not be the writer I am today if it were not for the confidence Mark Steinberg showed in me and my talent; he was the first to employ me to write his screenplay, *Fools & Mortals*. All *blame* must rest with him!

Everyone, family, friends, patrons and acquaintances who encouraged me to complete the screenplay and this book will find their reward in Heaven, I am sure. "Because they sure aren't getting fat on the wages I am paying them!" If they acknowledge, like I do, the story of Yeshua inspires everything. If "the world" will lean to Yeshua for all, nothing will collapse.

SOURCES

This book began as a screenplay narrative called *The Supernatural*. An account of all the miracles performed by Yeshua and recorded in the Gospels. The only part retained from this very early screenplay is the *Trial* which expanded to become the basis for my film narrative, the biopic about *Pontius Pilate*. At the time and now I use composite material provided by Matthew, Mark, Luke and John. The report of the *Trial* in this book, is not contradictory by complimentary, but complete in the details I researched. Since then, *The Chronological Gospels* was published and highly recommended for those of you who wish to gain an added Hebrew understanding.

While I estimate 75% of my book is actual recorded history, as a dramatization, I emphasize for the reader again, the chapter for the *Trial* is the 'purest' part of this book. The remaining 25% is of my own imagination and inspired too, historically credible and plausible.

Over the many years, since I started my 'new' life as a writer, I have read many books related to the subjects in some manner, *The Roman Empire, The Dead Sea Scrolls, The Lost Books of the Bible, The Sicarii,* etc. It was never my intent to write a book but remain a screenwriter. When moving multiple times trans-continental, Trans-Atlantic, latitudinal and longitudinally, I had to abandon my heavy libraries along the ways, leave them in the lofts of friends and never recover them. On one occasion, in a hurry to help my ailing mother, I left nearly every book I owned behind on the shelves. My friend David Norwood toiled to find a new home for them all: Thank you David. Dr. David Stephenson allowed me to read his special paper, a composite of the four Gospels so it may be understood as one account instead of the separated. The resources listed below represent the most recent references used but are a fraction of the total.

The Holy Bible, in particular the Gospels according to Matthew, Mark, Luke and John, mainly in the King James Version (KJV). However, I have read other translations.

The Chronological Gospels, Reconstructed and Annotated by Michael John Rood, which was most helpful to add the accuracy of dating and further my understanding of the dark antagonistic forces that attacked Yeshua. This book is the corrected KJV (CKJV).

Flavius Josephus, The Complete Works, translated by William Whitson, A.M. Flavius Josephus tells us *more* about Pontius Pilate's *activities* in Judea than the Gospels do! But the Gospels 'gave' me the true character of Pontius.

Caligula, The Corruption of Power, by Anthony A. Barrett. Thanks to this excellent book, I was able to springboard Pontius Pilate into place for this possible time. Pontius was *never* seen in the history books at this point, when Caligula was assassinated, ever before to my knowledge. Pontius is not mentioned in Mr. Barrett's book. My adaptation of Mr. Barrett's accurate *Caligula* was my preference to other known legends about Pontius. I can thoroughly recommend Mr. Barrett's book to you for the story of Caligula without my embellishment.

The Corrected King James Bible
THE CHRONOLOGICAL GOSPELS Michael John Rood
https://roodstore.com/collections/books-bibles

EPILOGUES

After Pontius Pilate was recalled to Rome to account for his annihilation of the Samaritans in Tirathaba, reliable accounts about him fizzle out: History does not record Pilate's ultimate fate. Speculation abounds. Legends are plentiful. The town of Vienne in France (called Gaul in Roman times) claims his burial place.

My narrative encompasses the real historic assassination of Caligula with the creative addition of Pontius and Claudia. No evidence exists to suggest Pontius was a conspirator. However, the physical evidence of Pilate's existence remains to this day.

The Physical Evidence

Discovered in 1961 in The Roman Theater, Caesarea Marittima, in Israel, a black limestone dedication states "Pilate, prefect/governor of Iudaea (Judea) Dated 26 - 37 Anno Domini," and a copy of which may be found on the site of the finding. The original is currently housed in the Israel Museum, Jerusalem, this was the first physical evidence of Pilate.

In 1968/1969 a ring was discovered with the inscription in Greek, "Pilato." Archeologists and historians believe this ring, which was thin and inexpensively made, would not have been worn by Pilate but by perhaps an administrator working for him in Judea.

The Roman Seal

At Joseph of Arimathea's tomb, the Garden Tomb, in Jerusalem, the broken iron rod and lead remains in the bed rock at the tomb to this day. A photograph may be seen on page 262 in *The Chronological Gospels,* Michael John Rood.

Dating the Trial, the Death and Resurrection of Yeshua

Agricultural and astronomical calculations are used to accurately date the days of Yeshua Ha Mashiach, His trial, and His resurrection. The dates have been computed by NASA in conjunction with the feasts and the Passover. For more information see *The Chronological Gospels* reconstructed and annotated by Michael John Rood and his team to correct the King James Bible. Yeshua was tried and crucified on a Wednesday and resurrected three days later, on Saturday, as stated prophetically.

The Sky at the Time of the Crucifixion

The movie will show the constellations in the darkened sky, midday to three o'clock in the afternoon, at the time of the crucifixion. The positions of the stars are verified by planetary calculations. The calendar may be seen in Michael John Rood's *The Chronological Gospels.*

The Ark of the Covenant

The Ark of the Covenant remains sealed in a cave directly below the crucifixion site as discovered by the American anesthesiologist and explorer Ron Wyatt. For more of Ron's amazing discoveries, including a blood analysis of Yeshua, see YouTube for the many audio-video accounts he and his family have posted.

Who were the first to be saved under The New Covenant?

Barabbas was first, the two 'criminals' alongside Yeshua on the cross were next. Today's Biblical scholars conclude that Pontius Pilate was saved. Pilate was an instrument of YeHoVaH, The New Testament, "the new deal for mankind," just like Caiaphas was, although he was too stubborn to let go of his old ways. No one person, a Roman, or group, the Jewish people, is to blame for the crucifixion. All of humanity takes responsibility. Someone had to fulfill prophesy written many years before these events. Pontius was so adamant about Yeshua's innocence, repetitively attempting to release Him during the course of the trial. Then Pontius demanded the sign YHVH (King of the Jews) be placed above his head in recognition of his deity. He stated emphatically, "What I have written, will always remain written."

All the above-mentioned visual elements will also be included in the finished film, *PONTIUS*.

ART DEPARTMENT

PONTIUS, PONTIUS REDEEMED & NO MAN CALLED ME COVER DESIGNS: Revised Edition, Special Edition & Universal Edition – Mark Darby Slater

Pontius Color Portrait - Universal Edition book COVER plus the *'Cinemascope'* (wide screen) Production Painting – *No Man Called Me* - Christine Harris

Diagrammatic Sketch - Location Map – Mark Darby Slater

Story Boards, etc. – *No Man Called Me* – Montgomery Triz

Figurative Characters & Portraiture by Caroline Slater
142. YESHUA
143. The younger Pontius
144. Pontius "after & before"
145. Pontius "after"
146. Claudia
147. Antonius
148. Antonius in helmet
149. Angels collage
150. Herod Antipas
151. Gaius Caligula
152. Shira
Carofineart.co.uk

NO MAN CALLED ME

Autobiography & Film development for *PONTIUS* search Amazon.com worldwide "No Man Called Me" Mark Darby Slater"

Personal & Private
Development of my film PONTIUS
NO MAN CALLED ME

Review by ANGELA V. JOHN, Professor of History, Biographer, BBC contributor

"... There are lots of goodies in your book. I enjoyed the historical explanations and the story boards ... I did find your "No Man Called Me' compelling. Your description of being seated at the front of Llandaff Cathedral in bright red trousers with tears streaming down your face is powerful! ... you tell your story well even though it is now far from being private and personal!"

Books by Angela V. John: Visit **http://www.angelavjohn.com/**

To become a Pontius Pilate The Movie patron
https://www.patreon.com/PontiusPilateTheMovie

go to the link above and you will see over 300 posts, stories, illustrations and the flow of development toward the goal, producing the film PONTIUS. Your small monthly gift brings me nearer to my objective. Tiny as it may appear to you, it helps me to underwrite my expenses. My ask of you is $1 a month or $5 or more if you can be so moved. It does not matter where you live, at home or abroad. All currencies are accepted.

In this particular instance, it will allow me to distribute some of these PONTIUS books as gifts. As indeed I have distributed many NO MAN CALLED ME books too. Your gift to me becomes a gift to them. The recipients will be people of industry or just those who maybe lost and in need to be found through the Biblical content herein.

My reward to date has been the joy of this dramatic creation and the adherence of this constancy to my purpose; the production of the movie! Please act now, become a patron, be in the inside, together, as we move forward. Thank you.

Mark Darby Slater

MarkDarbySlater@gmail.com

Film score by Arthur Donald Osborne www.artosbornemusic.com
To see more fine art by Caroline Slater www.carofineart.co.uk
To become a Pontius Pilate the Movie patron
https://www.patreon.com/PontiusPilateTheMovie
To be 'the' investor in Pontius the Movie contact Mark directly

Reviews

PONTIUS the SCREENPLAY

PONTIUS PILATE - a review by playwright LEE ROHE, ESQ., Attorney at Law

"It's captivating. I could feel the power of God when reading the tomb scene. The opening grips the reader (or film audience). God becomes a triumphant hero in rolling the stone back. The guards, blinded by the light, paralyzed with fear, shrink in the presence of a power beyond their comprehension.

The opening tells me immediately, as a member of the audience, that this story is going to have more spectacles in store. Before the theatre's lights dim and the film starts, we think we're going to watch a "biopic." But the opening scene promises more than non-fictional and fictional biography. It promises us we're going to also witness the grandeur and mystery of God's power.

The set up with Tiberius, Caligula, and Pilate in Rome instantly tells us what these characters are like. We also sense we're going to get a good dose of pagan life with all its abnormality and decadence. ..."

PONTIUS PILATE – a review by MARK STEINBERG, independent producer & Production Executive, EntrPro Productions.

"Exceptionally well written, an interesting take on a man who usually plays a minor part in the Passion dramas. A film based on this script will be a "winner" as skepticism is fairly placed. Certainly, will be a winner with both believers and non-believers. The motivations of the historical figures well depicted. Pontius Pilate becomes basically a decent person who made a mistake, justifies it reasonably and maintains his dignity, not at all like the evil individual depicted in so many films that deal with this era."

PONTIUS PILATE – Susan Izdepski, Hebrew Hieroglyphics Consultant.

"Historic fiction with historic and biblical truth!"

PONTIUS PILATE - Pastor Raymond L. Shockley, Church of God.

"Thought provoking! How many men are confronted with Jesus and do not know what to do with him? Mark this story needs to be told."

Rainbow Slicky Slide

Children discover the pot of gold at the end of the rainbow is the earth that God created. *Genesis 1.1*

Ages 3 – 8

Written by
Arthur Donald Osborne

Available from Amazon Books
TBN Trilogy Publishing

www.artosbornemusic.com

CAST OF CHARACTERS
in order of appearance

Antonius	Centurion, Claudia's cousin
Lefus	Centurion,
Pontius Pilate	The Roman Prefect
Yeshua Ha Mashiach	Jesus the Messiah
Barabbas	Leader of the Sicarii
The Arab	Magi
Dominicus	Paramour
Mus	Pontius's groom
Claudia Procula	Pontius's wife
Gaius Caligula	Tiberius Caesar's nephew
Tiberius	Caesar
Vinicianus	Senator
Caiaphas	The Temple High Priest
Shira	Hebrew servant
Annas	The Former Chief Priest
Nicodemus	Pharisee
Joseph of Arimathea	Pharisee
Herod Antipas	Son of King Herod the Great
Herodias	Antipas's 'queen'
Salome	Antipas's niece
Simon Peter (Kefa)	Disciple
Yehudas	Judas the Betrayer
Malcus	Servant
Mary	Mother of Yeshua
Mary Magdalen	Family Friend

Acilius, Tarraco, Creticus, Cicero, Roman Soldiers The Flagellators

Benjamin	Cook
Ingeniare	Roman Engineer
Yachanan	Disciple John
The Tribune	Senior Roman Officer
Aquila	Senator
Andrew	A Disciple
The Mad Man	Samaritan Leader

Marcellus	Envoy
Attending Academic	Astrologer and Physician
Gina	Dominicus's daughter
Chaerea	Tribune
Sabinus	Tribune
Livilla	Caligula's sister
Anicius Cerealis	Friend of Caligula
Sextus Papinius	Son of Anicius
Gnaeus Dominitius Ahenobarbus	Dominicus's husband
Caesonia	Caligula's wife
Drusilla	Caligula's daughter

"A Cast of Thousands"

The populations of Rome and Jerusalem, includes Roman dignitaries, Roman Soldiers, Street Urchins, The Sicarii - Dagger Men, The Jewish Council of Elders, The Sanhedrin, Pharisees, Sadducees, Priests, Scribes and Elders, Hebrew Crowds and Mobs, The Temple Guards and Temple Officers, The Money-Changers, The Samaritans, The Fighting Young Men of Tirathaba, The Old Men, Women and Children of Tirathaba, Roman Cavalry, Praetorian Guards, Caligula's tortured prisoners, Gladiators, Dancers from Asia, etc.

PONTIUS Book REVIEWS

"Masterful...characters flowed with ease ...fast-paced, intense ...Highly Recommended." COLONEL HOWARD, USAF, RTD.

"...every page exuding erudition ... the whole work presents the story with intrigue and momentum ... Pilate is shown in fresh light ... impactful." BRIAN SMITH, LEADER, KINGSHEART CHURCH, UK

"...will appeal to anyone ... I became engrossed ... Pontius became swept along by events ... I could not put it down ..." KEVIN BENNET, EDITOR, DLOC, UK.

"...cinematic style a completely new experience ...there isn't a more compelling plot ...enormous human interest...research is most impressive. Remarkable." DR. MATTHEW WHITE, UK.

"I was pleased to see how carefully you have followed the collated records found in the New Testament ... I found most intriguing the written portrait of Pilate which you have quite craftily created of him in chapters 14 through 21. I was also most gratified to find ensconced within these chapters the ... delineation of the avenue to salvation." DR. C. DAVID JONES, DOCTOR OF THEOLOGY, MINISTER, AUTHOR, INDIANA, USA.

"...the true meaning of events ...spiritual insights ...excellent reference ...enlightening and enjoyable." ARTHUR DONALD OSBORNE, COMPOSER, MINISTER, AUTHOR, TEXAS, USA

"Now I really want to see the movie." JEANNETTE SAUNDERS, MEDICAL RECORDS, FLORIDA, USA

"...based on a past life experience ... a complete and detailed depiction of the setting, time and people ...a witness." SUSAN L. ROHE, FLORIDA REGISTERED PARALEGAL, USA

"...a riveting tale told with great drama ...history, sex violence and even romance! The author moves the story swiftly to a climactic finish." KATRINA NICHOLS, JOURNALIST, MARKETER, CREATIVE WRITER, FLORIDA/PENNSYLVANIA, USA

"This book will suit believer or non-believer alike. ... visual and to the point. Pilate's wife Claudia, amazing." TERRY ST JEAN, TIMESHARE EXECUTIVE, FLORIDA, USA.

"...skillfully blends fact and fiction ... excellent relatable character development and lots of action makes this book an easy read." LINDA DEVORE, EDUCATOR, NEW JERSEY, USA.

"...this book had me hooked after the first chapter!! Well written, impeccably researched, and definitely had me rethinking much of my ingrained beliefs" – CELESTE M HOYT, BANKER, FLORIDA.

"...these reimagining leaves one with the feeling that this indeed is how it might have happened. Forget what you think you know and immerse yourself in this amazingly drawn portrait... I highly recommend it." - RANDOLPH V. ROME JR., U.S. COAST GUARD, RETIRED, FLORIDA.

"...As every page is turned, the reader is pulled into the environment and life of Pilate ... ultimate fate is covered by the authors clever use of historical data, expanded into conceivability ...thoroughly enjoyable." – GEORGE ZDANKO, INDUSTRIALIST, REDDITCH, ENGLAND.

"...The author has shown us a time from ancient history and his descriptive writing has brought the story and characters to life. Woven into the history, is the place of Jesus, known here by his Hebrew name with many nods to Ben Hur in his description of The Messiah. It has dramatic pace and many cinematic moments. We feel for the main character being caught up in this awful decision that is thrust upon him." ANNONYMOUS, HAMPSHIRE, ENGLAND.

"... It was riveting, and a little scary!! I appreciate the author's attention to detail, cross referencing passages of scripture, ... I could smell, taste, and feel the earthiness. I can't wait to see (and hear!) this movie. I know it will be stellar, and change the hearts of those who are ready and willing to empty themselves and to follow Yeshua, the risen Christ..." FLETCH WILEY, GRAMMY AWARD WINNER, TEXAS.

Christ For The Nations

To Whom It May Concern,

I thoroughly enjoyed reading Mark Slater's impressive classic, *PONTIUS,* which I will long remember. My name is Dennis Lindsay, President and CEO of Christ For The Nations in Dallas, Texas. CFNI, our Bible institute, has trained some 40,000 world changers over the last 50 years to share the good news of our Lord and Savior, Jesus Christ, to the nations. In addition, we presently have approximately 95 CFNI associated Bible schools around the world with some 50,000 additional graduates. I have personally shared with our students and staff the contents of *PONTIUS* and have been encouraging them to read the volume and look forward to the upcoming movie upon its release.

Since I have a love for God's Word and the nation of Israel, I have come to enjoy opportunities to read and learn more on the subject. My parents birthed Christ For The Nations in 1948, and our Bible institute in 1970. We continue to emphasize the importance of understanding the significance of the nation of Israel from a Biblical and future perspective. My wife and I have visited the Holy Land some 25+ times, leading tours year after year. My sister has been a resident of Israel for more than 50 years, where she and her family have served the Lord. We thank our God for the love of Israel that my parents passed on to us.

In reading the volume, my attention was captured immediately and would not be released until I completed the entire drama. The book was truly a spectacular adventure, full of action with historical and Biblical affirmation. I'm not sure which chapter drew me into its quest, but the interpersonal relationships were absorbing. I was drawn into the intimate life of *PONTIUS* and his wife Claudia. The connection in the trial between Barabbas and Jesus was extraordinary. I was truly amazed reading about Gaius Caligula and the supernatural events that transpired. It was a trauma that was breathtaking. Yet, the climax and concluding chapter must be one of the most amazing and unforgettable conclusions I've ever read. It brought tears to my eyes.

Screenwriter Mark Darby Slater has truly written and compiled an unforgettable story of the Messiah that no doubt will be played throughout eternity. I truly am happy to endorse *PONTIUS*, and I am looking forward to seeing the on-screen adaptation of this book. Christian audiences will support this movie, not to mention the number of individuals, like *PONTIUS*, who will surrender their lives to Yeshua.

Blessings,

Dennis Lindsay, D. Min

President & CEO

3404 Conway Street | Dallas, TX 75224 |
800.933.2364 | cfni.org

AUTHOR'S NOTES

This research-based novel contains *more* historic accounts and *more* Biblical facts and spiritual truths than it does my own fiction. My complete screenplay has been the foundation for this cinematically styled narrative.

Chapter Twelve, the Trial: The most accurate part of the book contains the chronological composite of all four Gospel writers: Matthew, Mark, Luke and John. Close examination of the whole trial period gives us the best insight into the character of Pontius, The Prefect of Judea and Samaria.

Flavius Josephus, the respected Hebrew historian of the period, gives us an account of Pontius's other activities and failures. Contemporary historians have contributed to my knowledge of characters, including Tiberius and Caligula.

Truth in context, *Pontius* gives extra insight into his life two thousand years ago to make it real and comprehensible in his space, his place, and in our time.

Mark Darby Slater
14th September 2020, Key West, Florida
Revised 1st January 2023, Lake Worth, Florida
Revised 1st February 2024

JESUS Yeshua & YeHoVaH
The Meaning

The historically correct Hebrew name YESHUA has been substituted for the Greek name JESUS. Yeshua means "to save, save alive, rescue." The name Jesus has no Hebrew meaning.

Similarly, where appropriate, the Hebrew name YeHoVaH, used in preference to the generic English "God" or "Lord." YeHoVaH means "the peg or nail, the hole, the hand, revealed to save."

This makes the obvious connection between Father YeHoVaH and Son YESHUA. Amazingly, the proper reading of YeHoVaH (Lord) in The Old Covenant adds prophetic meaning.

The use of ELOHIM (God) appropriately identifies His Son, Yeshua. The interchange of the proper names may enhance our understanding. The Holy Spirit, RUACH HAKODESH in Hebrew, to complete The Holy Trinity.

YeHoVaH should not be confused with Jehovah's witness or any other doctrine or denomination.

For more information relating to the ancient and modern use of YeHoVaH see *The Chronological Gospels*, Michael John Rood, page 28.

Pontius Redeemed, a biographical non-fiction novel, with action, drama and adventure. With historical and Biblical correctness in context.

BIBLIOGRAPHY

PAGES	REFERENCES		CHAPTERS
5	Pages 235 Expanded in Chapter 12	CKJV KJV	TAVAK Into The Midst
33	The War of The Jews* Exodus 20:4	Flavius Josephus	4 GRAVEN IMAGES
44	The War of The Jews*	Flavius Josephus	5 SIT DOWN
62 68 69 71	The War of The Jews* Luke 7: 2.3.4 Matthew 8:7 Luke 7:6 Matthew 8:8 Matthew 8:9} Luke 7:8} Luke 7:9 Luke 7:7	Josephus KJV	6 FORGIVENESS & HEALING
74	Page 161	CKJV	7

74	John 7:45 John 7:47.48	KJV	PLOT
75	John 7:49		
	John 7:51		
	John 7:52		
	John 11:43		
76	John11:47		
	John 11:48		
	John 11:49		
	John 11:50		
	John 11:53		
86	Page 194	CKJV	9
87	John 12:13	KJV	PROCESSIONS
	Luke 13:39		
	Luke 19:40		
95	Matthew 21:13 Mark 11:17	KJV	10 TEMPLE
99	*Begin* Page 234	CKJV	11 VISION
100	Matthew 26:49	KJV	11

100	26:50 26:55 Matthew 26:55} Mark 14:49} Luke 22:53} Luke 22:53 Matthew 26:54 & Mark 14:49}		VISION
101	Matthew 26: 55	KJV	11/12 VISION & TRIAL
	Unabridged	*Gospels*	12 TRIAL
	Drama	*Complete*	*The composite*
			Accurately
105	John 18:4.7 18:5 18:5 18:8 Luke 22:51 John 18:11	In narrative sequence	12 TRIAL

106	Matthew 26:52} 26:53} John 18:11		
107	Matthew 26:61 & Mark 14:58} Matthew 26:62 & Mark 14:60}		
108	Matthew 26:63 Matthew 26:64 & Mark 14:62} Matthew 26:65 & Mark 14.63} Matthew 26:66 & Mark14:64}		
109	John 18:19 John 18:20/21 18:22 18:23 Luke 22:64 & Matthew 26:67} Mark 14:65, Matthew 26:67.68 & Luke 22:64}		

109	Matthew 15:1 Luke 22:67 Luke 22:67.68.69 Luke 22:70		
110 112	Luke 22:71 Luke 23:29 Luke 23:30 & John 18:30} Luke 23:31 & John 18:36}		
113	Luke 23:31 & John 18:31 Luke 23:2 Luke 23:2 Luke 23:2		
114	John 18:29 Mark 1:2, Luke 23:3 & John 18:33} John 18:34		

	John 18:35		
	John 18:36		
	Matthew 26:53		
	John 18:36		
	18:37		
	17:38		
116	Luke 23:4 & John 18:38}		
	Luke 23:5		
	Mark 15:5		
	Matthew 27:14		
	Matthew 27:13 & Mark 15:4}		
	Mark 15:5		
	Mark 15:4		
117	Luke 23:8		
	23:9.10		
118	Luke 23:11.12		
119	Luke 23:14		
	Luke 23:15		
	Matthew 27:19		
120	Mark 15:9		

	Luke 18:40		
	Matthew 27:19		
	Matthew 27:19		
120	Matthew 27:20		
121	Matthew 27:22 & Mark 15:12}		
	Matthew 27:22 & Mark 15:13}		
	Mark 15:14		
	Matthew 27:13 & Mark 15:4}		
	Mark 15:5		
	Matthew 27:14		
125	Mark 15:9 & John 18:39}		
	Mark 15:11		
	Mark 15:13		
126	Luke 18:40		
	Mark 15:18		
	Luke 23:18		
127	Luke 23:22		
129	Luke 23:16		
	Luke 23:21		

130	John 19:4		
131	John 19:5		
	John 19:14		
132	John 19:15		
	John 19:15		
	John 19:15		
133	John 19:6		
	19:7		
	19:8		
	19:9		
134	John 19:10		
	John 19:11		
	John 19:11		
	John 19:12		
	John 19:12		
135	John 19:15		
	John 19:15		
	John 19:15		
	John 19:15		
136	Matthew 27:24		
	Matthew 27:24		
	Matthew 27:24		

137	Matthew 27:25 Isaiah 53:7		
149	Luke 23:34	KJV	
151 152	John 19:19 adapted Luke 23:38 23:38 adapted		
153	John 19:21 John 19:22		
156 157	John 19:30 Adapted:- Mark 15:39 Mark 15:44		
160	John 19:31 John 19:33		
162 162 163 170	Page 258 Matthew 27:63 Matthew 27:64 Matthew 27:52.53 Matthew 28:3 Mark 9:3	CKJV	14 THEFT

171	Matthew 28:4 Matthew 28:6 & Mark 16:6		
172	Matthew 28:7 & Mark 16:7		
173	Matthew 28:12 28:13 28:14 Page 261		
	The War of the Jews*	Flavius Josephus*	16 AQUEDUCT
201 203	Adapted John 3:1-8	KJV	17 MASSACRE
	The Antiquities of the Jews*	Flavius Josephus*	
	Caligula The Corruption of Power*	Anthony A. Barrett*	18 EMPEROR GOD
	Caligula The Corruption of Power*	Anthony A. Barrett*	20 ASSASSINATION
	Read John 3: 1-21	KJV	21 SAVIOR

	& *No Man Called Me, personal & private,* episodes 11,12 & 13, an explanation for physiological, psychological and emotional understanding	Author Mark Darby Slater's book	
	---------------	*Pontius Redeemed*	
	John 19:10 John 19:11	Chapter 21, Page 258, in the context of the Trial, seen in Chapter 12, Page 138.	The moments of redemption for Pontius. His personal experiences of salvation.

KJV – King James Bible
CKJV – Corrected King James Bible - *The Chronological Gospels,* Michael John Rood

Paginations in the above chart may shift, caused by at least three electronic transfers of files; Word to PDF to the publisher's file. Every edition, this one being the third, may also change the page numbers. Approximately 158 Biblical quotes appear in this book. I beg your forgiveness if the above table is not in alignment. However, the quotations in context are 'perfect' - just like me!!!

Pontius Story Boards

Montgomery Triz created the following story board samples while reading my feature-length screenplay for *Pontius*. My writing-style implies many of the camera angles. Therefore, Monte had no difficulty interpreting the script.

Ultimately the film director will visualize how to shoot each scene. Hundreds of illustrations will be rendered by the story board artist in discussions with the director. This in turn will assist the cinematographer and help everyone to set-up the space, lighting and the equipment they will need to execute the filming, shot-by-shot, scene-by-scene.

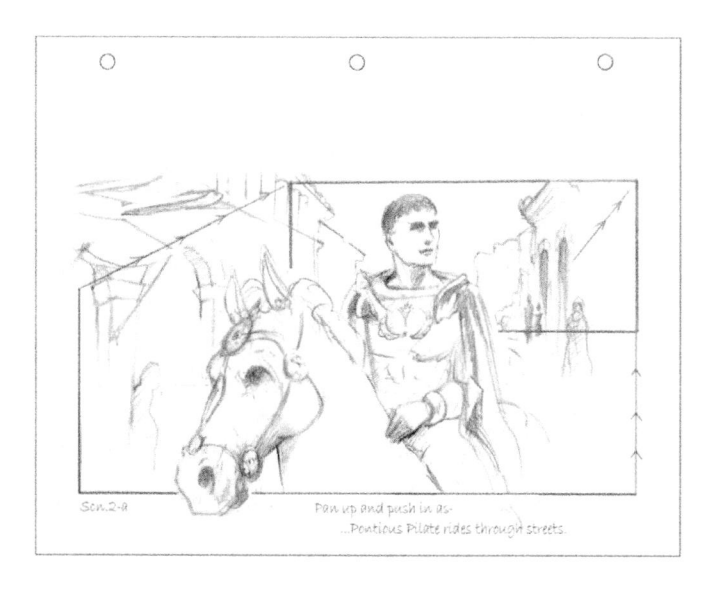

Chapter 1

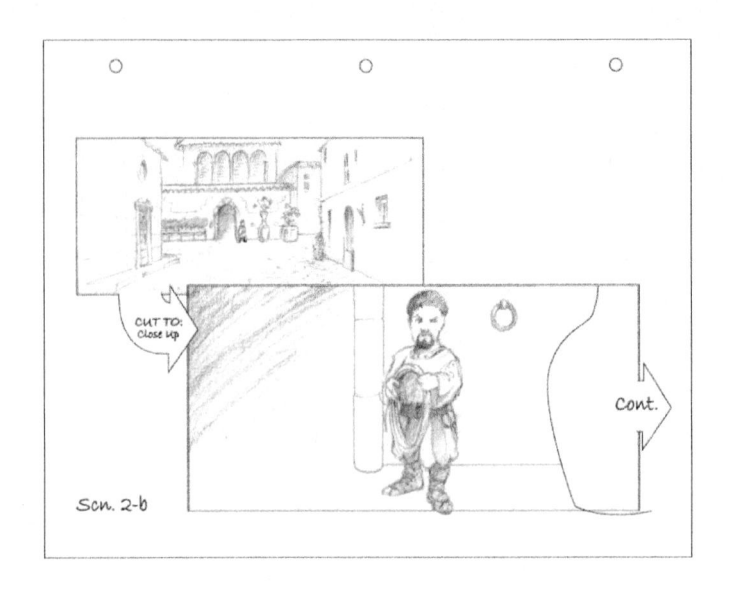

CUT TO:
Close up

Cont.

Scn. 2-b

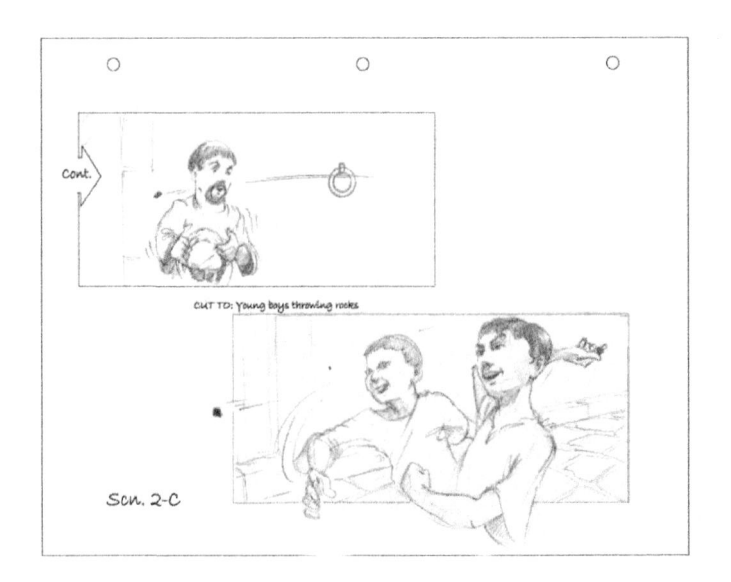

Cont.

CUT TO: Young boys throwing rocks

Scn. 2-C

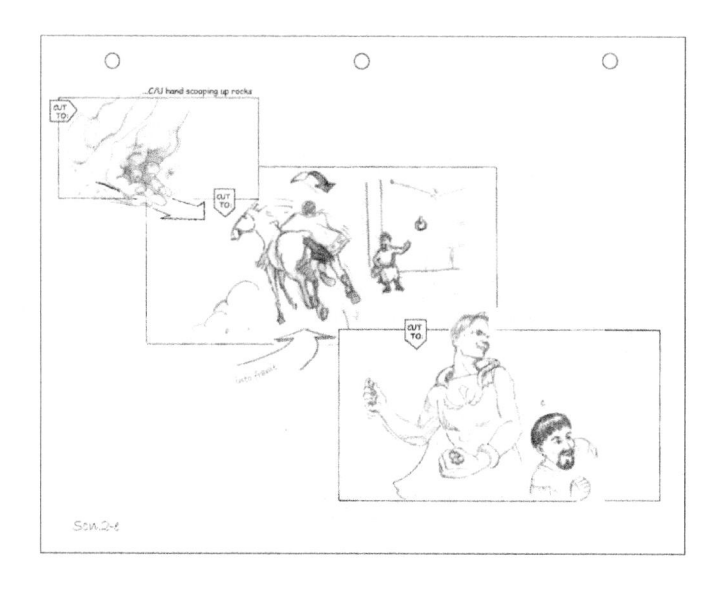

CUT TO: Pontious gallops in to frame preparing to dismount

Scn. 2-D

...C/U hand scooping up rocks

Scn. 2-E

Scn.2-f — Follow boys as they turn and run

Scn.2-g — Pontious Pilate enters the villa. Mus leads the horse away.

CUT TO:

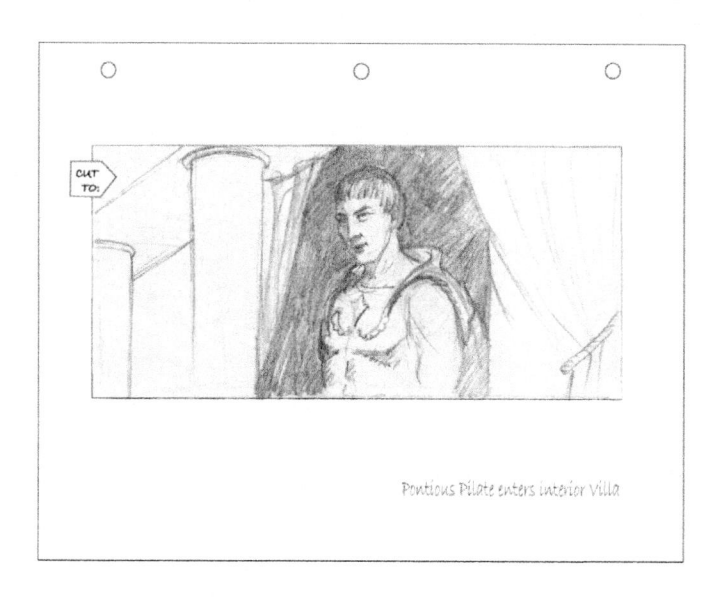

Pontious Pilate enters interior Villa

CUT TO:

P.O.V. slowly lowers and pushes in as Claudia walks out of the shadows towards Pontious.

CONT.

Scn. 3-A — pan to the right

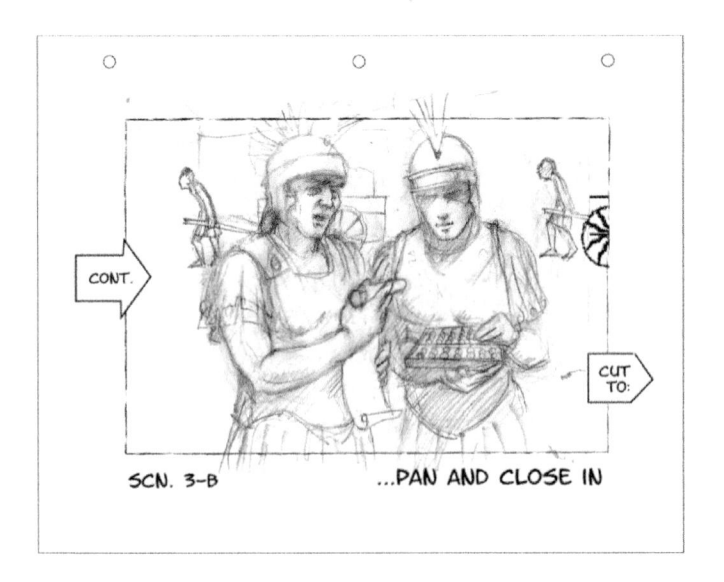

SCN. 3-B — ...PAN AND CLOSE IN

Chapter 3

Chapter 6

Scn. 28-D

Chapter 13

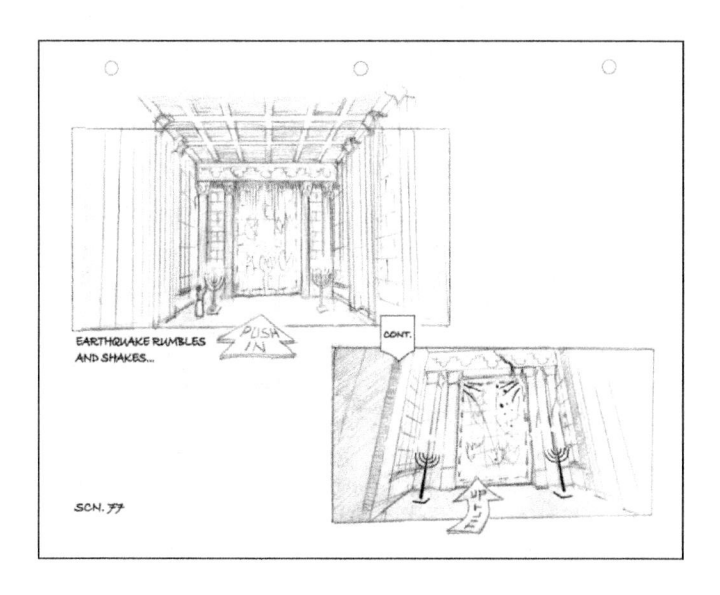

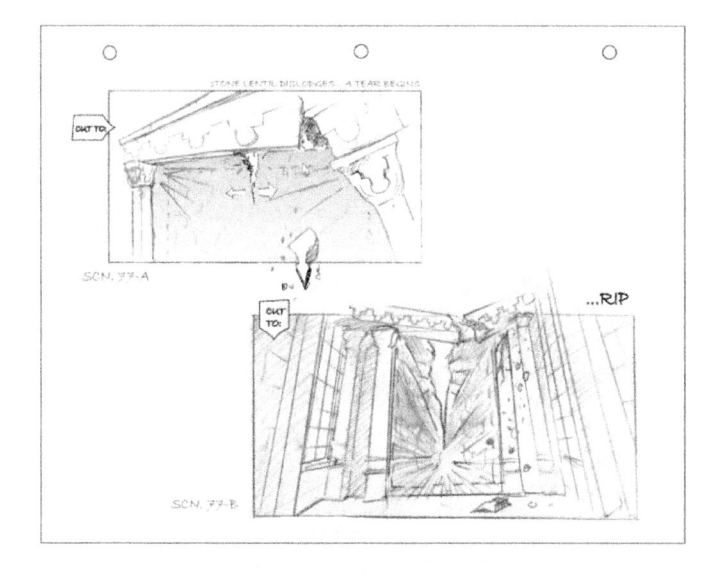

Chapter 15

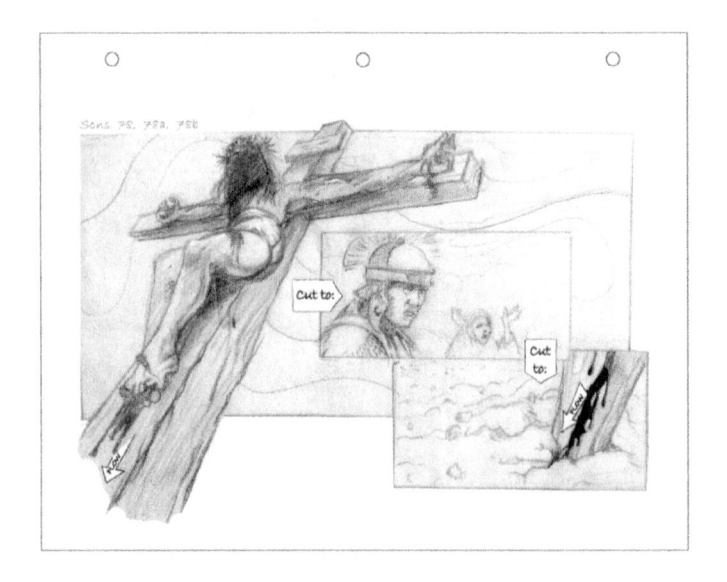

Scn. - 98-B Exterior Garden and Tomb - Night

    The "seal," as it is referred to in The Bible, actually an iron rod, dipped in lead, and driven through a hole in the 'round stone door' into the bedrock of the tomb. The rod shown will placed correctly in production.

Emperor Gaius Caligula by Montgomery Triz

High Priest Caiaphas by Montgomery Triz

Chapter 17

Scn. 127 - C

Montgomery Triz also illustrated the cover of my book, *Landing on Clouds,* (available on Amazon Books), in color. The screenplay, *Saving Elena*, was written with Henry Villate. In Monte rendered many story boards which appear in this book "...Clouds" based on extraordinary events in Key West, Florida, from 1930 to 1940. Described as "a gem" ...

Artistic Impressions of the HERALDIC PLAQUES rendered by *CaroFineArt.co.uk.* These samples are imaginings of the plaques Pontius errected at the Antonia Fortress in Jerusalem. *Pontius* Chapters 4, 5 and 6.

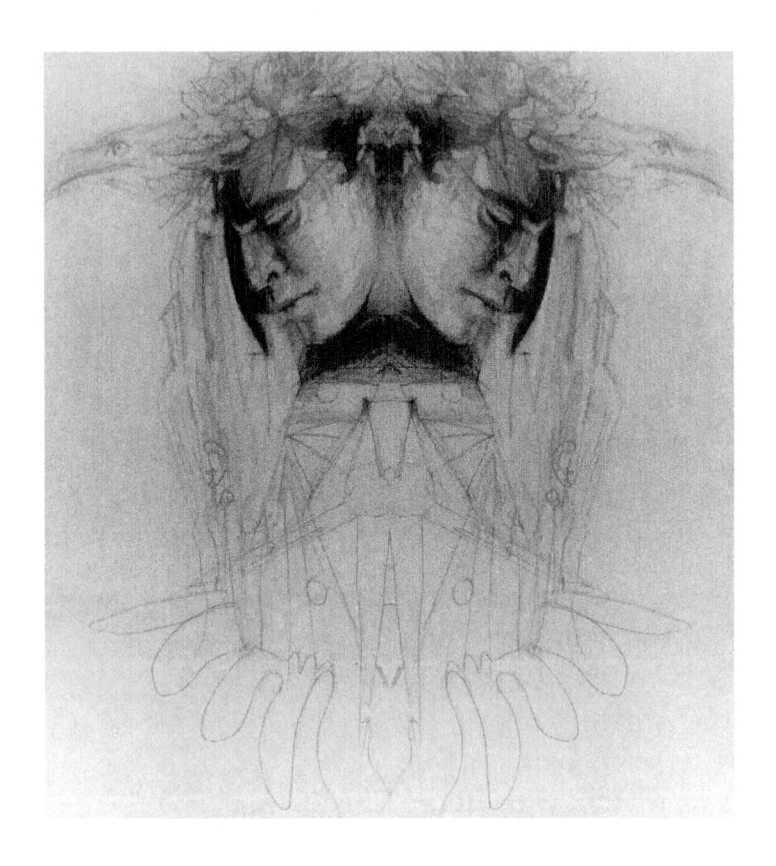

The above, originally in sepia. Caroline also drew portraits of principal characters which appear between Chapters 12 and 13, *Pontius Redeemed.*

Caroline originated this painting in colour.

Shown here in black and white.

Tiberius Caesar, imagined by Caroline.

Pontius Redeemed

Chapters 2, 15 and 18.

Yeshua, a Metamorphosis
by Caroline
as Pontius looks on

Writing *Pontius*

AFFIRMATION

The composite, chronological compilation of the four Gospel accounts amalgamates to give us the best insight we have into Pilate's character. In addition, the historic accounts of Flavious Josephus widen our knowledge. Josephus's history provides an example of Pontius the compassionate man who allows many Hebrews to escape his sword. Perhaps never before told with such completeness, this gives the best insights into Pontius's character.

When writing *Pontius*, it was necessary to develop his character with actions and words. In chapter 2 Pontius exclaims, *"You may believe whatever you like…"* after he saves Caligula's life. This element was written by me circa 2018 to convey Pilate's belief system and liberalisms and lack of pagan Roman dogma. When coming to the Trial of Yeshua Pontius states, *"I see no fault in this man"* in chapter 12. This shows The Prefect had a philosophy and capacity for leniency, which he applied to Our Yeshua's case.

According to the historian J. O. Kinnerman, D.D. (*Celt, Druid & Culdee,* Isabel Hill Elder, page 54) Pontius did not follow Roman paganism or Greek philosophy. I did not discover this until I received the above-mentioned book as a gift from a friend. That Pontius was educated in part by The Druids of the western isles, Britain, perhaps Wales. This I did not learn until 2023, five years after I concocted and used a writer's tool (chapter 2) to reveal a part of Pontius Pilate's character. My conjecture became a supportable fact. The Prefect could be compassionate at times. Therefore, I hold this discovery, thanks to Kinnerman and Elder, as it solidifies who Pontius really was, who I imagined him to be. The way I constructed Pontius, considered fair and reasonable, supports the Gospel writers too.

Mark Darby Slater, February 2024

Pontius™

Redeemed

And the Lord answered me and said, "Write the vision and make it plain upon tablets, that he may run that readeth it. For the vision is yet for an appointed time, but at the end it shall speak and not lie; though it tarry, wait for it; because it will surely come."

Habakkuk Chapter 2 Verses 2 & 3

Please add your review to Amazon Books, search Mark Darby Slater, *Pontius Redeemed.*

Printed in Great Britain
by Amazon